EDWIN

MUIR

Poet, Critic and Novelist

Margery McCulloch

EDINBURGH UNIVERSITY PRESS

Transferred to digital print 2013

Edinburgh University Press Ltd
22 George Square, Edinburgh

Typeset in Linotron Garamond 3 by
Photoprint, Torquay, and
printed and bound by CPI Group (UK) Ltd, Croydon, CR0 4YY

A CIP record for this book is available
from the British Library.

ISBN 978 0 7486 8308 6

The publisher acknowledges subsidy
from the Scottish Arts Council towards
the publication of this volume.

Contents

Abbreviations

A	*An Autobiography*
B	*Belonging*
CP	*Complete Poems*
ELS	*Essays on Literature and Society* (revised edition 1965)
EP	*The Estate of Poetry*
M	*The Marionette*
PA	*The Present Age*
PT	*Poor Tom*
SF	*The Story and the Fable*
SJ	*Scottish Journey*
SL	*Selected Letters*
SN	*The Structure of the Novel*
SS	*Scott and Scotland* (Polygon Books edition 1982)
TB	*The Three Brothers*
WM	*We Moderns*

Wherever practicable, quotations will be referenced in the text by title abbreviation and page number.

Acknowledgements

Acknowledgement is made to the Muir Estate, to Faber & Faber and to Hogarth Press for permission to quote from Edwin Muir's writings.

I should also like to thank Edwin Muir's nieces, Irene Abenheimer and Ethel Ross, for their friendliness and willingness to talk to me about Muir and his family; and Dr Roger Stephenson of the University of Glasgow for his helpful comments on my translations from the German poets referred to in Chapter 2.

Finally, I owe a debt of gratitude to Alexander Scott (1920–89), who first gave me encouragement in my work on Edwin Muir and other writers of the Scottish Renaissance, and who himself contributed much to Scottish literature as poet, scholar and teacher.

Introduction

Edwin Muir belongs chronologically to a remarkable group of writers of the modernist period which includes T. S. Eliot, Ezra Pound, the late Yeats, D. H. Lawrence, James Joyce and Virginia Woolf; and in the Scottish context Hugh MacDiarmid, Neil M. Gunn and Catherine Carswell. Yet, despite his significant achievements as European poet, critic, translator and to a lesser extent novelist, Muir stands somewhat apart both from the main thrust of literary modernism in the early decades of the century and from the contemporaneous movement to revitalise Scottish writing, which was given impetus primarily through the innovative Scots-language poetry of Hugh MacDiarmid. As an Orkneyman, Muir always had an ambivalent attitude to what he called his 'second country'[1] and its national identity conflict, although his own critical writings contributed much to the Scottish cultural debate. His own earliest literary influences were from English poetry of the Romantic and Victorian periods. He comments in his autobiography that when he first began to write poetry in Europe at the late age of thirty-five, he 'was too old to submit myself to contemporary influences' and had 'no technique' by which he could give expression to his imagination's promptings. 'There were the rhythms of English poetry on the one hand, the images in my mind on the other. All I could do at the start was to force the one, creaking and complaining, into the mould of the other' (A 205). Placed alongside the innovative work of an Eliot or MacDiarmid, Muir's early poetry is eclectic, uncertainly self-reflexive in subject matter and on the whole neutral in form and language. His European affinities were with German Romantic and post-Romantic poetry as opposed to the French Symbolist poetry which excited the interest of Eliot and MacDiarmid and the influence of Flaubert in the fiction of Joyce and Woolf.

From a formal perspective, then, Muir does not readily fit into the modernist context. Yet, as Helen Gardner commented in a memorial lecture in 1960, in the circumstances of his own life he was 'deeply involved in the long crisis of this century' while he was also 'through his own personal distresses, profoundly affected by the revolution in our whole conception of human personality brought about by the genius of Freud and Jung'.[2] If modernism is an awareness of historical and cultural crisis relating to innovation and change in the sciences and in philosophical thought, as well as being seen as a period of exceptional experimentation in the arts, then there can be no doubt that Muir has his place in this movement. Ironically, the symbolism and greater stylistic emphasis in the best of his mature poetry from *The Narrow Place* (1943) onwards bring him closer formally to literary modernism at a time when that movement is usually considered to have passed.

Muir's life story has been well documented through his own accounts in his autobiography *The Story and the Fable* (1940) and its revised and extended version *An Autobiography* (1954), and in Willa Muir's *Belonging* (1968). A brief outline will therefore suffice here. He was born in the Orkney Isles in 1887 and from the age of two until seven lived on his father's farm, the Bu, on the small Orkney island of Wyre. As we see from his autobiography, Wyre and the Bu became the scene of the child's earliest intimations of place and identity and provided the inspiration behind many of the themes and images in his adult poetry. However, although Wyre made such a strong impression on Muir's childhood imagination, the family did not remain there for long. The high rental demanded by an 'improving' landlord drove them when Edwin was seven to a less good farm on Wyre, then to a poor farm on Mainland island. They finally gave up farming altogether, moving first of all into the town of Kirkwall and subsequently emigrating to Glasgow in 1901.

The family's experiences in industrialised Glasgow proved to be even more devastating than their lack of farming success in the virtually pre-industrial environment of Orkney. Within four years of their arrival, both parents and two elder brothers were dead, and the remaining members of the family – Edwin, two sisters and a brother – decided to go their own ways. At the age of eighteen, Muir found himself alone in Glasgow, physically unwell and psychologically disturbed, under-educated and poorly employed and with no apparent prospect of improving his situation. Looking back in later years on that traumatic transplantation, Muir commented:

> I was born before the Industrial Revolution, and am now about two hundred years old. But I have skipped a hundred and fifty of them. I was really born in 1737, and till I was fourteen no time-accidents happened to me. Then in 1751 I set out from Orkney for Glasgow. When I arrived I found that it was not 1751, but 1901,

and that a hundred and fifty years had been burned up in my two
days' journey. But I myself was still in 1751, and remained there
for a long time. All my life since I have been trying to overhaul
that invisible leeway. No wonder I am obsessed with Time.
(*SF* 263)

Although Muir in the end 'climbed out of these years' (*A* 110) to
become an acknowledged critic and poet, to the end of his life he
continued to be something of a displaced person. He and his wife Willa
had no settled home after their marriage in 1919 but divided their time
between travel and work in Europe and residence in England and, often
more unhappily, Scotland. Throughout his life, Orkney remained for
him the 'north' to which what Willa Muir called 'his secret compass'
always pointed (*B* 113). He never again lived for an extended period in
the islands, although he visited Orkney regularly for holidays. He died
in hospital in Cambridge on 3rd January 1959 and was buried in the
nearby village of Swaffham Prior where he had lived since returning
from a visiting professorship at Harvard in 1956. His life and work are
commemorated by a plaque in St Magnus Cathedral in Kirkwall,
designed by his fellow Orkneyman, the artist Stanley Cursiter.

Many people come to Edwin Muir's poetry by way of the depiction of
his Orkney childhood in *An Autobiography*, which communicates the
intensity and timelessness of the young child's experience while
blending with this the adult man's reflection on its significance for him
and for the way we all live our lives. His account of his childhood is
therefore not a direct, unmediated transmission of incident and emotion
but, as in Wordsworth's *The Prelude*, the communication of emotional
response and vision articulated by the adult who selects and orders his
memories, at times stepping outside the remembered childhood as adult
observer and commentator, at others using his adult skill with language
in order to bring the child's perceptions alive for the reader. Muir was
strongly influenced by Romantic poetry and thought, and his account of
his childhood on Wyre is therefore part of that wider Romantic
discourse. He is at one with Wordsworth and Blake in his intuition of
the essential truth of the child's world picture, of its strength-giving
virtue. He tells us that the child has

> a picture of human existence peculiar to himself, which he
> probably never remembers after he has lost it: the original vision of
> the world. . . . Certain dreams convince me that a child has this
> vision, in which there is a completer harmony of all things with
> each other than he will ever know again. (*A* 33)

Muir's memories, however, are earthier, more ritualistic and at times
more surrealistic than anything one would find in Wordsworth.

Alongside timeless descriptions such as that of his father sowing the grain – 'the sun shone, the black field glittered, my father strode on, his arms slowly swinging, the fan-shaped cast of grain gleamed as it fell and fell again' (A 32) – we have accounts of the pig-sticking ritual at the farm, a surrealistic dance of death which is yet cruelly sobering in the way it forces us to consider our dependent relations with the animal world. We experience with the child his horror and revulsion at the insects which formed 'the underworld of my little underworld' and which terrified him

> with thoughts that could never be penetrated, inconceivable aims, perverse activities. . . . I could never bear to touch any of these creatures, though I watched them so closely that I seemed to be taking part in their life, which was like little fragments of night darting about in the sun. (A 21)

Here, we are in the world of MacDiarmid's 'Country Life' with its 'golochs on the wa', / A craidle on the ca'' – a poem which fascinated the adult Muir and which he described as having 'an almost fantastic economy, a crazy economy which has the effect of humor and yet conveys a kind of horror'.[3]

Many of Muir's Orkney memories are of animals, as in the following account of an encounter with the horses brought in from the fields by his father and cousin Sutherland:

> I stood trembling among their legs, seeing only their great bearded feet and the momentary flash of their crescent-shaped shoes flung up lazily as they passed. . . . Everything about them, the steam rising from their soft, leathery nostrils, the sweat staining their hides, their ponderous, irresistible motion, the distant rolling of their eyes, which was like the revolution of rock-crystal suns, the waterfall sweep of their manes, the ruthless flick of their cropped tails, the plunge of their iron-shod hoofs striking fire from the flagstones, filled me with a stationary terror and delight for which I could get no relief. (A 22)

In this splendidly vital prose description, reminiscent in its imaginative energy of Blake's 'The Tyger', we find the inspiration behind Muir's early poem 'Horses' from *First Poems* (1925) and the mystical regenerative symbolism of the late poem 'The Horses' from the *One Foot in Eden* collection of 1956.

Muir tells us that his 'passion for animals comes partly from being brought up so close to them, in a place where people lived as they had lived for two hundred years; partly from I do not know where'. There is thus mystery but no sentimentality in his depiction of the relations between human and animal worlds. For him, 'the animal world is a great impersonal order, without pathos in its suffering. Man is bound to it by necessity and guilt, and by the closer bond of life, for he breathes the same breath'. We have therefore this recognition of a bond enacted optimistically (as in 'The Horses') and the simultaneous acknowledgement of the power of ritual to transform guilt and effect a reconciliation between worlds. In his experience, 'a farm is such a carnival of birth and death, there is no wonder that it should frighten a child'. Yet 'a child could not grow up in a better place than a farm; for at the heart of human civilization is the byre, the barn, and the midden' (*A* 48, 53, 36).

As with his recognition of the bond between human and animal worlds, so Muir's Orkney childhood was the source of his awareness of the essential relationship between the everyday and the unseen world, what he was to call in his autobiography 'the story and the fable'. Although he did not overtly make use of his father's stories of witches and the supernatural in his poetry, these stories arose from a timeless folk imagination in which 'there was no great distinction between the ordinary and the fabulous'. And to the growing child, Orkney was a place where 'the lives of living men turned into legend' (*A* 14). His playground was the cairn of the legendary Cubbie Roo's Castle; his mother's story of her terrified girlhood vigil with the shipwrecked Danes, neither side able to communicate with the other, had the quality of an episode from a saga. Religion, too, united the mundane and the supernatural in the child's imagination. The date of the millennium was a subject of regular speculation in his family, as were King David's relationship with God and the question of whether Elijah ascended to heaven in a chariot of fire or a whirlwind. To the child, his parents seemed 'fixed allegorical figures in a timeless landscape', where 'the image "mother" meant more than "woman", and the image "father" more than "man"' (*A* 24–5). In these childhood 'memories', we can recognise the source of that sense of the 'beyond' and of the relationship between the ordinary and the fabulous, the mundane and the transfigured which lies at the heart of Muir's poetry and at the heart of the poetry of the Romantic period.

Muir's affinities with Romantic ideology leads into his relationship with post-Romantic writers such as Matthew Arnold who, like Muir in his sudden transition from Orkney to Glasgow, were faced with the intrusion of the Victorian city into their predominantly rural childhood and non-urban education at the universities of Oxford and Cambridge. Pope's optimistic eighteenth-century view of technological development – 'Rich Industry sits smiling on the plains'[4] – had quickly been superseded by Wordsworth's concern over the herding of people into cities and factories to meet the demands of the new industrial machine, with the result that they required more and more artificial stimuli to activate their imaginations. Victorian poets experienced even more keenly these Romantic period forebodings as urban and rural worlds increasingly came hard up against each other, and none of the major poets of the time succeeded in coming to terms with the city experience. Tennyson's late vision of Camelot ultimately disintegrated into the chaos of the contemporary city while, among other manifestations of a divided psyche, Clough's *Dipsychus* pointed to the disintegrating effect on the human personality of the industrial division of labour, an insight which anticipated Muir's. Arnold's advice to the Scholar-Gypsy was to 'fly hence',[5] and he himself saw that flight as being in a return to the universal values and timeless themes of the classical world.

Muir's response to modernist experience had much in common with that earlier uneasy Victorian response to urbanisation and industrial-isation. He eschewed both the embracing of nihilism which he believed he perceived in a writer such as D. H. Lawrence and the preoccupation with form which was characteristic of many visual artists, musicians and writers of the time. Like Clough, Muir saw the machine not as life-freeing but as enslaving, as the logic of machine-functioning began to be applied to the organisation of human society. Like Arnold, he sought to establish a sense of philosophical equilibrium by returning to traditional values in the face of contemporary crisis, both traditional values as represented by the classics as in Arnold but also, for Muir, the traditional cooperative and communal values which he associated with his Orkney childhood. As with fellow Scots MacDiarmid and Gunn in their attempt to revitalise Scottish life and literature, this emphasis on traditional values gave Muir's involvement with philosophical modernism a more overt regenerative aim than was the norm. The shock of his own first-hand experience of a clash of cultures set him on a quest for understanding and integration more typical of the Romantic and immediate post-Romantic periods, a quest which he defined memorably in *An Autobiography* as the three mysteries of 'where we came from, where we are going, and, since we are not alone, but members of a countless family, how we should live with one another' (*A* 56).

While autobiography is to some extent an input in the work of all writers, Muir's creative writing and the pattern of his life came together more overtly than is often the case, and most critics of his poetry have foregrounded this relationship, especially with regard to the opposition between the Orkney and Glasgow life experiences and the imagery of Eden and the Fall in the poetry. While accepting the importance of the autobiographical element and deploying this where relevant, I would wish to enter a caveat in regard to the distinction between early and mature poetry. In Muir's early poetry, as in his novels and some early essays, he is more obviously struggling to come to some understanding of the tragedies in his own life and to find some way forward for himself in the face of determinism and mortality. In some early poems, the imagery derives from dream visions induced by psychoanalysis and is therefore difficult for the lay reader to interpret, being of interest primarily from a psychoanalytic perspective. In others, the imagery is personal in an autobiographical way and again depends upon an *hors-texte* context for satisfactory understanding. In the mature poetry, however, this external dimension is no longer intrusive. While an autobiographical element may still be present in the inspiration or interpretation of a poem, knowledge of this is not essential for understanding. It is one possible layer of meaning among several and can be introduced or ignored as the reader wishes. Subject matter and imagery now validate themselves. In discussion of Muir's poetry, I have therefore spent less time on the early collections from *First Poems* to *Journeys and Places* and have concentrated more closely on what I would see as the mature poetry from *The Narrow Place* to *One Foot in Eden*.

Muir has on the whole been pushed to the periphery in historical accounts of early twentieth-century literature in English, most probably as a consequence of his stylistic apartness from modernist influences. In his Preface to the 1965 *Selected Poems*, T. S. Eliot commented that while he himself 'went through a period of concentrating my attention on experiment in metric and language', such involvement with technical innovation was never 'a primary concern with Edwin. He was first and foremost deeply concerned with what he had to say.'[6] On the other hand, Muir has always attracted a supportive group of readers and scholars, and among them they have put together a considerable body of edited collections and critical articles and books about his life and work, thus consolidating his place in the literary history of the period.

While this new study is much indebted to these previous scholars, it diverges in several ways. Since I would see Muir's poetry, criticism and novel-writing all as part of his ongoing discourse about the meaning of human life, and since I believe that both his criticism and his novels deserve more recognition than they have previously had, I have included individual chapters on Muir as novelist and as critic. As mentioned above, I have also given more attention to the poetry from 1943 onwards and have followed Christopher Wiseman's lead in foreground-ing where relevant the *stylistic* maturity of the later poetry, thus attempting to maintain a more even balance between form and subject matter in analysis and assessment. So far as the earlier poetry is concerned, I have given prominence to the influence of German Romanticism in *First Poems*, an influence which is not readily perceptible from the small group of poems reprinted in the *Collected Poems* of 1960 but which is clear from *First Poems* itself. I have also included a chapter on Muir and Scotland, since this is an aspect of Muir which has largely been ignored in previous studies. The neutral linguistic surface of his poetry, the relative absence of specifically Scottish subject matter and his prominence as reviewer and critic in English periodicals have meant that the Scottish dimension in his life and work has not been sufficiently appreciated. Yet, as I hope this study will show, he himself was deeply influenced by his Scottish background, not least by the deterministic philosophy of Calvinism against which he fought in both poetry and prose; and his critical writings about Scotland, together with his portraits of Scottish society in books such as *Scottish Journey* and his Glasgow novel *Poor Tom*, have contributed much to our understanding of Scottish culture. This therefore seemed to be an area worthy of fuller consideration.

Finally, I have tried to give emphasis to Muir as a poet of this single, disunited world of the twentieth century. Many readers have been attracted to Muir because of the spirituality they find in his work, a spirituality absent in much literature of our period. Previous critics have on the whole foregrounded this transcendental, spiritual aspect, and Elizabeth Huberman and Peter Butter have placed especial emphasis on his Christianity. On the other hand, my own interest in Muir has been principally as a poet of the mundane world, who, as a result of the tragedies in his own life, has been able to enter into the experiences of the displaced and of those who suffered during the Second World War and through the communism of the postwar period, and to evoke powerfully our search for meaningful values in this crisis-ridden century. Once again it seems to me that this sublunary Muir has been to some extent sidelined in favour of the Muir of Eden and the world before the Fall. While still keeping in view Muir's preoccupation with the eternal 'Why?', I will therefore in my discussion of the poetry focus on poems and interpretations which seem to me to emphasise the third of Muir's 'mysteries': 'how we should live with one another', rather than those which seem to have a more overtly religious or transcendental message. For me, Muir is at his best as the spokesman for this 'difficult land' which is yet 'our home'.

NOTES

1. Edwin Muir, 'Nooks of Scotland', *The Listener*, 16 January 1958, p. 120.

2. Helen Gardner, *Edwin Muir: The W. D. Thomas Memorial Lecture*, delivered at the University College of Swansea on 8 December 1960 (Cardiff: University of Wales Press, 1961), p. 7.

3. Edwin Muir, 'The Scottish Renaissance', *Saturday Review of Literature*, 31 October 1925, p. 259.

4. Alexander Pope, 'Windsor Forest', *Alexander Pope's Collected Poems*, ed. Bonamy Dobrée (London: Dent, 1924), p. 23.

5. Matthew Arnold, 'The Scholar-Gypsy', *The Poetical Works of Matthew Arnold*, ed. C. B. Tinker and H. F. Lowry (London: Oxford University Press, 1950), p. 261.

6. T. S. Eliot, Preface, *Selected Poems: Edwin Muir* (London: Faber & Faber, 1965), p. 10.

One

The Early Poetry 1925–37

From 1907 when it came under the editorship of A. R. Orage, the *New Age* was one of the liveliest and most influential of English cultural periodicals in the pre-1914 period. Orage himself has been described as 'a great artist in literary encouragement',[1] and among aspiring writers whose first published work appeared in his journal were Katherine Mansfield, John Middleton Murry, Herbert Read and T. E. Hulme, together with Edwin Muir and his fellow Scot C. M. Grieve (Hugh MacDiarmid).

Muir first came to prominence in the *New Age* as critic and prose-writer. While living in Glasgow, he had contributed a series of Nietzschean aphorisms on the modern period, and these were published as *We Moderns* in 1918 under the pseudonym of Edward Moore. Shortly after he moved from Glasgow to London with his wife Willa in 1919, Orage offered him a post as his assistant on the journal.

We Moderns was successfully received in America, and as a consequence the *Freeman* magazine offered Muir a contract. This enabled him to leave London for Europe in the summer of 1921, and it was during this first European sojourn that he began to write poetry. Muir later said of their stay in Prague: 'It was the first time since I was fourteen that I had known what it was to have time for thinking and daydreaming . . . I began to learn the visible world all over again' (*A* 189). And in Dresden, where they stayed after Prague:

> I seemed at last to recover from the long illness that had seized me when, at fourteen, I came to Glasgow. I realized that I must live over again the years which I had lived wrongly, and that every one should live his life twice, for the first attempt is always blind. (*A* 192)

From Dresden they went to Hellerau, where Willa Muir taught for a time in A. S. Neill's international school. There, under the influence of a German friend, Ivo von Lücken, he began to explore the poetry of

Hölderlin, and at the age of thirty-five he himself began to write poetry. Of this time, he comments: 'I began to write poetry simply because what I wanted to say could not have gone properly into prose. I wanted so much to say it that I had no thought left to study the form in which alone it could be said.' And when in later years he thought back to what had influenced him, he could 'only think of the years of childhood which I spent on my father's farm in the little island of Wyre in Orkney, and the beauty I apprehended then, before I knew there was beauty'. Now, 'these years had come alive, after being forgotten for so long' (A 206).

Muir had previously made verse contributions to the *New Age* between 1913 and 1916, but this was his first serious attempt at writing poetry. He was later dissatisfied with this early work, which was published as *First Poems* by Leonard and Virginia Woolf at the Hogarth Press in 1925. Only six of the original twenty-four poems were reprinted in the *Collected Poems* of 1952, and nine were included in the posthumous *Collected Poems* of 1960.

To appreciate fully the apprentice nature of *First Poems* and Muir's preoccupations in the collection, one must return to the original 1925 edition as opposed to the small selection from the work given in *Collected Poems*. The poems reprinted in 1952 and 1960 show a more consistent standard of technical attainment, some of this due to later revisions by Muir. Their themes are more clearly defined and can be related more readily to the themes of the later work. Thus 'Childhood' establishes the tranquillity and security of the childhood vision of Wyre which was to be so significant a part of Muir's Fall imagery, while 'Ballad of Hector in Hades' is the first example of the employment of the material of Greek legend to give objective form and universality to his personal search.

The original 1925 collection, on the other hand, is very much an eclectic work where one finds him essaying various modes in the attempt to find his own voice. Poems such as 'An Ancient Song', 'Betrayal' and 'Anatomy' offer a strongly visual element in their imagery and the kind of conceits associated with Elizabethan and Jacobean poetry. The sonnet 'An Ancient Song', in its characterisation of Bereavement, transforms such conceits into what would become typical Muir imagery:

> Bereavement which, by deathless Memory teased,
> Pores o'er the same, forever-altered track,
> Turns, ever on the old lost way turns back;
>
> (*CP* 12)

He was later to reuse these lines in *Variations on a Time Theme*.

Six poems, two of them in Scots, are ballad imitations. None, apart from 'Ballad of Hector in Hades', is truly successful. 'Ballad of Rebirth' and 'Ballad of Eternal Life' ('Ballad of the Soul') are based on the dreams which Muir experienced during psychoanalysis in London when he was working with the *New Age*, but the imagery calls for therapeutic interpretation, and the dreams themselves are more powerfully communicated in the prose of *An Autobiography*. The theme of 'Ballad of the Nightingale' was later to find more imaginative expression in 'The Transfiguration' from *The Labyrinth*.

The attempt to employ the Scots language in 'Ballad of the Monk' and 'Ballad of the Flood' is also undistinguished. There is in it none of the vital creativity to be found in Hugh MacDiarmid's use of Scots; no attempt to penetrate to the psychological heart of the language or to reshape it towards contemporary needs. Perhaps the difference between the Norse-influenced Orkney speech and Lowland Scots made Muir feel as much of an outsider in the use of Scots as he claimed in his *Freeman* article 'A Note on the Scottish Ballads' that all Scottish writers were in the use of English: 'No writer can write great English who is not born an English writer and in England'.[2] In neither Scots nor English did he explore the creative, allusive potentiality of vocabulary which one finds in MacDiarmid or, to disprove his strictures on the writing of great English, in the work of the Irishman James Joyce.

There is also little imaginative development of theme in these Scots ballads. 'Ballad of the Flood' is enlivened only by the transformation of Noah into the leader of Calvin's Elect:

> 'To hell the haill warld gangs this day,
> But and my folk sae gude.
> Sail on, sail on till Ararat
> Lifts up aboon the flood.'
>
> *(CP 33)*

'Ballad of the Monk', on the other hand, would appear to be a Gothic re-enactment of Nietzsche's concept of eternal recurrence, as the 'sma banes' of the 'snaw-white skeleton' (*CP* 28–9) reassemble themselves in an eerie anticipation and reversal of the scattered bones of T. S. Eliot's 'Ash Wednesday'. It is surprising that he never collected what one could argue is his most successful poem in Scots, 'Ballad of the Black Douglas', published in *Scottish Chapbook* in July 1923. This poem is a fine ballad imitation which catches the elliptical, suspenseful quality of ballad narrative. It is rhythmically satisfying, and here the Scots language context provokes both imaginative imagery and genuine pathos:

> 'O what is this that lies sae white?
>   Is't may plucked frae the tree?'
> 'It's the king's body that's covered a'
>   Wi' the white leprosy.'. . .

And after Douglas has departed to carry the dead king's 'hameless heart'
on his last longed-for journey:

> Black Douglas went beyond the sea,
>   His lance within his hand,
> But he never cam' wi' his gude men
>   Into the Holy Land.

> He never saw Jerusalem's
>   Green shaws and flowery braes.
> His king and he lie side by side
>   In a far lanely place.
>
> *(CP* 281–2)

This 'broukit bairn' from MacDiarmid's *Chapbook* deserves a wider
audience than it has had hitherto.

One significant feature of the original *First Poems* is the influence of
German Romanticism on Muir's early poetry. This is an influence
characteristic of his work as a whole, which consistently displays an
interest in and affinity with German thinkers and writers. Nietzsche
was the philosopher to whom he turned as a young man in Glasgow in
the attempt to understand and order his sense of personal dislocation;
and the prose works *We Moderns* and *Latitudes* exhibit the not altogether
fortunate effects of that influence. Goethe and Heine were other German
influences in his Glasgow days, and to these he added during his stay in
Hellerau the poetry of Hölderlin and Hofmannsthal.

In *An Autobiography*, Muir speaks of 'a sickly, graveyard strain in
Heine's poetry' which lay alongside his 'exquisite wit' and of his own
obsession with this element in Heine's work during his period of
employment in the foul-smelling bone-factory office in 'Fairport'
(Greenock): 'I battened on tombs and shrouds' (*A* 144). Although his
direct attempts to emulate Heine would appear to have been limited to
the early poems published in the *New Age*, the *Sehnsucht* of Heine's
poetry and of Goethe's 'Kennst du das Land?' from *Wilhelm Meisters
Lehrjahre* dominates several of the poems in *First Poems*. This theme
of longing is itself, however, mediated through yet another early
influence: that of English Romantic and Victorian poetry. *An
Autobiography* makes clear Muir's sense of being at one with Wordsworth
in relation to the idea of childhood as a period of innocence and intense

visionary experience. In addition, his account of his reading material as a young man in Glasgow points to an involvement with poems of the Romantic and post-Romantic periods which were concerned both with visionary experience and with the need to transcend human suffering. He tells us: 'I was enchanted by *The Solitary Reaper*, the *Ode to a Nightingale*, the *Ode to the West Wind*, *The Lotus-Eaters*, and the chorus from *Atalanta in Calydon*' (*A* 99). The time spent as an apprentice chauffeur in Ayrshire 'is associated with Rossetti and Swinburne' (*A* 100). Yet while the relationship with Wordsworth was to remain a constant, positive element in his work, the influence of Victorian poets such as Rossetti and Swinburne, as with Heine, left less fortunate traces. The keen sense of life which tempers Keats's longing for transcendence in 'Ode to a Nightingale' can in Rossetti be transformed into a self-reflexive nostalgia, a quality in evidence in several of these early Muir poems.

All these influences from Muir's early reading are explicitly or implicitly present in the poems of longing in *First Poems*. 'The Lost Land', through its title, most openly points to Goethe's 'Kennst du das Land?', a poem which for Muir held the essence of the sense of *Sehnsucht* found in Romantic literature.[3] In both poems, the exiled speaker expresses longing for the lost land. In Mignon's song, the idealised forms of the vision communicate themselves firmly to speaker and reader – 'die Zitronen blühn, / Im dunkeln Laub die Goldorangen glühn'; 'Es glänzt der Saal, es schimmert das Gemach, / Und Marmorbilder stehn und sehn mich an: / Was hat man dir, du armes Kind, getan?'[4] (the lemons blossom / the golden oranges glow in the dark foliage; the hall gleams, the room shimmers with light / And figures of marble stand and look upon me: / What have they done to you, poor child?). Muir's poem, on the other hand, is based on one of the dreams which came with psychoanalysis, and in it the object of the longing is itself nebulous and unreliable as in a dream: 'The houses waver towards me, melt and run'. There is an empty, deserted quality about the longed-for landscape when it finally comes into focus: 'The doors wide open where the wind comes in'; 'The still church standing lonely on the mound, / The leaning tombs which slumber with no sound'. And, suddenly, another look dispels the dream vision entirely:

> I look again. Alas! I do not know
> This place, and alien people come and go.
> Ah, this is not my haven; oft before
> I have stood here and wept for the other shore.

> (*CP* 4)

Here, not only is the homeland lost through exile, but the fact of its ever having existed is under question. There is a similar ambiguous note in the generally more positive vision of 'Houses', where even amid the remembrance of previous security there is potential menace. The land here is 'the green estranging land'; the rooms are 'closed', with walls which 'listening stand'; the child is 'half-afraid'; 'the empty fields spread waste and wide'; 'those distant houses shine with grief and mirth' (*CP* 6–7).

First Poems communicates strongly Muir's own sense of personal and philosophical insecurity, an insecurity which, paradoxically, was allowed free expression as a result of the sense of safety and freedom engendered by his stay in Hellerau. Reading his account of his years in Glasgow in *An Autobiography*, one can understand how the *Sehnsucht* of Goethe and Heine took such a hold on his imagination: 'Nur wer die Sehnsucht kennt / Weiss, was ich leide!'[5] (Only someone who really knows longing / Knows what I suffer!). Yet, in these early poems, Muir's exiled speakers are more vulnerable than their German counterparts. Mignon's yearning has a firm focus; Heine's young men yearn after the unattainable lost love, but there is a toughness about their longing which seems to come from self-awareness and is communicated through an irony directed towards self and situation. When Muir attempted Heine's irony in his *New Age* poems, it resulted in a synthetic witty cruelty entirely foreign to his future work. In 'A Question to my Love' he asks:

> How dost thou win repose's balm,
>   When I must toss on life's wide sea?
> Is it wisdom makes thee calm,
>   Or, dearest, mere stupidity?[6]

In *First Poems*, it is not clever cruelty but the pain of longing which predominates. In addition, the poet's anguished plea for an understanding of life's mystery in the closing lines of 'Reverie' evokes Hofmannsthal's questioning in 'Ballade des äusseren Lebens'. Muir's speaker asks:

> Why do we walk with muted footsteps round
>   In this strong trance called life from which none wake? . . .
> Why do I wait still with my foolish pain?
>   All, all at last must take their sorrow home.

> (*CP* 10–11)

Similarly, for Hofmannsthal:

> Und Kinder wachsen auf mit tiefen Augen,
> Die von nichts wissen, wachsen auf und sterben
> Und alle Menschen gehen ihre Wege.[7]

> (And children grow up with deep eyes
> Understanding nothing, grow up and die
> And all people go their way.)

First Poems of 1925 is an apprentice collection in the context of Muir's work as a poet, yet it is more significant for an understanding of both the themes and the formal qualities of his later poetry than the nature and limited number of the poems reprinted in *Collected Poems* of 1960 might suggest. Through the reprinting of poems such as 'Betrayal', 'Ballad of Hector in Hades', 'Ballad of the Flood', the European settings of 'Autumn in Prague' and 'October at Hellbrunn' and the Wordsworthian 'Childhood', one is made aware of the range of influences on Muir referred to earlier in this chapter, but in *Collected Poems* these are subsumed into a recognisable 'Muir voice', either as a consequence of the nature of the poem selected, or because of revisions and excisions made later by Muir. One does not find the extreme philosophical insecurity or the German influence which are present in the original collection. While one is aware in 'Childhood', for example, of the affinity with Wordsworth and the Wyre of *An Autobiography*, the poem's pointing towards integration, to a world where 'the sky fitted the earth and the earth the sky' (*A* 33), takes one also into the world of Hölderlin and his 'Da ich ein Knabe war':

> Da spielt' ich sicher und gut
> Mit den Blumen des Hains,
> Und die Lüftchen des Himmels
> Spielten mit mir.[8]

> (I played there safe and good
> With the flowers of the grove,
> And the sky's heavenly breezes
> Played with me.)

The collection is therefore especially important for an awareness of this German influence on Muir's work, something which may well have contributed to the slow growth in his poetic reputation in a period when the predominating European literary influence was French. Yet the preoccupation with *Sehnsucht* as in Goethe and Heine and the striving for transcendence and integration to be found in Hölderlin were both to become significant elements in Muir's exploration of the Fall theme which, as George Marshall suggests, has in Muir's hands more to do with exile than with sin.[9] And although Muir would appear not to have been familiar with the poetry of Rilke at this period of his life, the psychological situation presented in many of these poems of exile is that described by Rilke in his definition of *Sehnsucht*:

> Das ist die Sehnsucht: wohnen im Gewoge
> Und keine Heimat haben in der Zeit.[10]
>
> (That is what longing is: to dwell in a state of flux
> And to have no homeland in the world of Time.)

This is a theme which continued to preoccupy Muir in his later work, and its prominence in these German poets is no doubt one of the reasons why he found himself so drawn towards German literature.

In addition, the sense of personal dispossession and dislocation so much in evidence in the ambivalent imagery of *First Poems* establishes Muir's credentials as a poet of the dispossessed, spiritually and materially, of twentieth-century Europe. Muir's Fall theme was no mere adopted theme. *First Poems*, in its original version, is equally important with *An Autobiography* for an understanding of his life and work, and it is good that it is now more readily accessible through Peter Butter's recent edition of the *Complete Poems*.

Chorus of the Newly Dead, the long poem which followed *First Poems*, was published by the Hogarth Press in 1926. This was to a significant extent also a product of the Hellerau experience, having been begun during Muir's stay there and, according to Willa Muir in *Belonging*, 'continued, with excitement and pleasure', when they returned to Neill's school after the *Freeman* ceased publication (*B* 102). Sections of the poem appeared in MacDiarmid's *Scottish Chapbook* in August 1923, and some were translated into German during Muir's stay in Hellerau by a young German woman, Gerda Krapp, a eurythmics student at Neill's school.[11] The impulse behind the poem would seem to have been in part a desire to overcome the romantic subjectivity which had characterised *First Poems*. Muir wrote to Sydney Schiff (the novelist Stephen Hudson) that he 'wished to get a certain pathos of distance in contemplating human life' and that the characters in the *Chorus* would be

> types like the Saint, the Beggar, the Idiot, the Hero, the Mother, the Rebel, the Poet, the Coward, and they will all give some account of their lives as they see it from eternity, not in Heaven or in Hell, but in a dubious place where the bewilderment of the change has not been lost. (*SL* 37)

Unfortunately, as Muir himself later recognised, these 'types' remain abstract entities. They cannot arouse our interest or empathy because they themselves have no individual life. Apart from a few touches in 'The Harlot' of a recognisable everyday world ('the traffic's beat', the 'weak lamps' of 'the darkening street', the 'dark and dusty well' of the 'toppling tenement' (*CP* 42–3), the suffering of the victims in the *Chorus* is played out without human context. The attempt to contemplate life at a distance has resulted in a divorce from human life as we know it. Instead of creating an atmosphere of 'mystery and wonder at the life of the earth' as he had indicated in the letter to Sydney Schiff, the poem makes one of the first explicit statements in Muir's poetry of the obsession with determinism which was to colour much of his future work:

> It was decreed. We cannot tell
>   Why harlot, idiot or clown
> Lived, wept and died. We cannot spell
>   The hidden word which drove them down.
>   (*CP* 43)

The comment on the Idiot's sense of alienation:

> He did not know the place, the alien throng;
>   The light was strange to him, bound by the awe
> Of a once-broken long-forgotten law
>   (*CP* 39)

anticipates, as did the poems of longing in *First Poems*, the imagery of dispossession and loss in later Fall-theme poetry.

There is a space of eight years between *Chorus of the Newly Dead* and Muir's next sizeable collection of poems, *Variations on a Time Theme*. These eight years were, however, filled with experiences which, although on the surface they might be thought to have delayed his development as poet, were in fact an integral part of that development.

During this period, Muir gained an increasing reputation as critic, prose-writer and, in association with his wife, translator. A commission to translate Feuchtwanger's *Jud Süss* had provided them with the opportunity to live in France between March 1926 and May 1927, and this successful book was followed by the translation of Feuchtwanger's *Die hässliche Herzogin*. In the early 1930s, they began work on Hermann Broch's *Die Schlafwandler* with its theme of the inevitable break-up of civilisation in contemporary Europe, a disturbing book which re-awakened Muir's latent neurotic fears. Their translation of Kafka's *Das Schloss* appeared in 1930, followed by *Beim Bau der chinesischen Mauer* in 1933. As with his earlier discovery of German poetry, the involvement

with Kafka's work uncovered an affinity between Muir's own
preoccupations and those of Kafka's novels, and may well have helped
give definition to his 'lost way' themes. His own fiction, and especially
the novels *The Three Brothers* and *Poor Tom* with their considerable
autobiographical input, helped him to explore the unresolved tensions
of his past in fictional form. All these prose-writing activities
contributed to the emergence of the mature poetry of the 1940s.

In the mid-1930s, however, Muir was still seeking the way forward
as poet. *Variations on a Time Theme* is a bleak collection. It opens with a
striking passage of imagery which derives from his experience of the
diseased countryside around Glasgow in the early years of the century,
imagery which he used again in the Glasgow chapters of *An
Autobiography*. In the prose work, he describes the walk along

> a cinder path leading past a pit, beside which was a filthy pool
> where yellow-faced children splashed about. Tattered, worm-
> ringed trees stood round it in squalid sylvan peace; the grass was
> rough with smoke and grit; the sluggish streams were bluish
> black. (*A* 92)

Here, in *Variations*, the speaker asks:

> How did we come here to this broken wood?
> Splintered stumps, flapping bark, ringwormed boles,
> Soft milk-white water prisoned in jagged holes
> Like gaps where tusks have been.
>> Where did the road branch? . . .
> > > > > > > (*CP* 51)

The ten poems of the collection were not originally written as a linked
sequence, but appeared individually over a period of time in
publications such as *The Listener* and *The Spectator*. They are united,
however, by their poet's obsession with themes of time and mortality,
preoccupations also of the novels *The Three Brothers* and *Poor Tom*. After
the opening passage, it is T. S. Eliot's voice which frequently echoes
through the collection and fragments of imagery more characteristic of
'Gerontion', *The Waste Land* and 'Ash Wednesday' which give form to
Muir's questioning and his sensation of futility and loss. In many of the
poems, human time is seen as a 'place of disaffection', thus anticipating
Eliot's later 'Burnt Norton', but there is little sense of a 'time after'
which will bring positive release and recompense.[12] Instead, there is the
Nietzschean concept of eternal recurrence, the 'sad stationary journey' of
'generation after generation' (*CP* 52) and the futility of the time present
in which each generation is similarly imprisoned: 'we have known /
Only this debris not yet overgrown'; the 'dead stones / Among dead

stones' (*CP* 56, 55). 'Time' in these poems would appear to be both the restrictive, predestined fate of Calvinism and the very fact of mortality itself which seems to deny lasting significance to human lives. 'Time is a sea' in which we face 'Death's bullying gale'. Time, not the human being, 'is the fisher. / Me he will catch and stuff into his net / With mortal sweepings, harp and banneret.' Time is also 'a fire-wheel whose spokes the seasons turn, / And fastened there we, Time's slow martyrs, burn' (*CP* 59). Muir's torment is in some ways still the torment of Heine's awareness of the impermanence of human achievement – 'Ja, zu Grund muss alles gehn . . . was gut und gross / Und schön, das nimmt ein schlechtes Ende'[13] (Yes, everything must go to ruin . . . whatever is good and great and beautiful must come to a wretched end) – but the focus of his longing is his search for the integration between human and eternal worlds found in the poetry of Hölderlin: 'im Arme der Gotter wuchs ich gross'[14] (I grew in the arms of the gods).

Perhaps the most successful poem in the *Variations* collection is 'IX', which first appeared in *The Spectator* of 22 December 1933 entitled 'The Dilemma'. It incorporates the themes of Time, and, more tentatively, the Fall, and reintroduces that Indifference which plagued Mansie Manson in the novel *Poor Tom* and which was to reappear as the 'Interceptor' in *The Labyrinth* of 1949. In this poem, one notices again the affinities with Elizabethan and early seventeenth-century English poetry apparent in *First Poems*, and indeed the third stanza reuses, with minor alterations, the striking and characteristic evocation of the passion of Bereavement from 'An Ancient Song'. Yet, despite its assured beginning, the poem is ultimately unresolved. The implication that suffering is justified by the need to keep indifference at bay through pity suggests Muir's continuing inability at this point in time to come to terms with his own past experiences and exemplifies a lack of philosophical resolution typical of the collection as a whole.

The final collection to be discussed in this review of Muir's early poetry is *Journeys and Places*, which occupies a pivotal position between the apprentice and mature work. Although published in 1937, it is, like *Variations*, a product of Muir's experiences in the late 1920s and 1930s, six of its twenty-four poems having been published by the Samson Press in 1932, and five of these six poems – 'The Trance' (later entitled 'The Enchanted Knight'), 'Tristram Crazed' ('Tristram's Journey'), 'The Stationary Journey', 'The Fall' and 'Transmutation' ('The Threefold Place') – having been written, according to Willa Muir, about 1928 (*B* 146).

In the early 1930s the Muirs lived in Hampstead, where they met many of the young, politically-oriented poets of the time, while from

1935 until 1942 their home was in St Andrews in Scotland. Although in periodical articles and prose writings such as *Scottish Journey* (1935), *Social Credit and the Labour Party* (1935) and *Scott and Scotland* (1936), Muir effectively pursued questions of immediate national, political and literary relevance, one does not find in his poetry of the time the overt political and social concerns which characterised the work of English writers such as Auden, Spender and Day Lewis, and which are present also in MacDiarmid's poetry of the 1930s. While critics such as John Holloway and Thomas Crawford have argued persuasively for a consideration of poems such as 'Troy' and 'A Trojan Slave' as political poems of the interwar period, I would see Muir's primary preoccupation in these poems, and in *Journeys and Places* as a whole, as being still with 'the eternal problem' of the search for self-knowledge and spiritual significance in an apparently meaningless universe, an issue which he first raised in *We Moderns* and which had dominated his poetry up to this point.

Journeys and Places exhibits to the greatest extent so far Muir's use of myth and legend to embody that search, a search given definition variously through themes of the Fall of Man and the Fall of Troy, through Arthurian legend, through literature and history. His attitude to the material of poetry is still that of the critic of *We Moderns* and *Latitudes*. In the latter, he had complained that in the work of modern writers art is 'blasted, and from inside, by a necessity to insinuate into it something less triumphant than itself: the "problems" of our time' (*L* 68); while in *We Moderns* he had, like Arnold in the nineteenth century, contrasted unfavourably the artistic criteria of the modern period with those of the ancient Greeks. For Muir,

> the Greeks did not aim at the reproduction but the interpretation of life, for which they would accept no symbol less noble than those *ideal* figures which move in the world of classic tragedy. To the Greeks indeed, the world of art was . . . a symbolizing of the deepest questions and enigmas of life. (*WM* 15–16)

This is similar to his view in the 1930s as he contemplated the politically-oriented work of the Auden generation. He tells us that 'a new generation had appeared from a country which I had never guessed at', which 'appeared to belong in a specific way to the present' (*A* 232–3). Their 'new poetry had left the immemorial hopes behind it' (*A* 235). In contrast, Muir felt himself to belong to that lost generation which should have spanned the gulf between the pre-1914 period and the 1930s, but whose survivors could not make contact with the new world:

> The generation to which I belong has survived an age, and the part of our life which is still immobilized there is like a sentence broken

off before it could be completed; the future in which it would have
written its last word was snatched away and a raw new present
abruptly substituted. (*A* 194)

The tragedy of Muir's generation was also the tragedy of his own
individual journey, and *Journeys and Places* continues his attempt to find
a way to relate his past to the alien present.

Technically, *Journeys and Places* is much in advance of the earlier
collections, despite linguistic remnants of undigested romanticism
which linger in phrases such as 'eld's frosted hair'; 'the feathery tomb
bursts open, / And yellow hair is poured along the ground / From the
bent neck of Time' (*CP* 65, 85). The much-praised but ultimately
enigmatic 'Enchanted Knight' is an amalgam of Keats's 'La Belle Dame
Sans Merci' and Heine's 'Nacht lag auf meinen Augen', which Muir
read in his Glasgow days in George MacDonald's translation in the
Canterbury Poets edition of Heine. In *An Autobiography*, Muir tells of
the influence which this particular poem of Heine's exerted on him
during the time he worked at the bone factory in Greenock, when the
state of neurotic arrestment symbolised in the dead man's inability to
respond to his lover's call seemed to match his own emotional condition
(*A* 144–5).

As in *Chorus* and *Variations*, predominant themes in this collection
are the philosophical ones of time, mortality and immortality,
determinism and recurrence, and the apparent futility of our human
journey when attempted in such a restricted context. The preoccupation
with a Calvinist view of existence as a predestined journey whose end no
human act on earth can modify comes increasingly into focus. For the
protagonist in these poems, human beings are subject to 'a force
unknown / That neither answers nor yields'; 'you could not leave these
fields' (*CP* 91, 90). 'The Hill' reshapes Muir's *Latitudes* essay 'North and
South' and Heine's 'Ein Fichtenbaum steht einsam' in its use of the
north / south antithesis as symbolic of rejection or election on Judgment
Day. Its speaker finds that 'he does not know . . . if, arriving, he will
be / With the bright divers never still, [the chosen] / Or on the sad
dishonoured sands' of the rejected northerners (*CP* 68).

Poems in the 'Journeys' section of the original edition describe
movements from one mental state to another in addition to any physical
journey undertaken, as in 'Tristram's Journey', where the movement is
into and out of madness. The first poem in the collection, 'The
Stationary Journey', demonstrates what Willa Muir describes as 'an
indulgence in one of the occupations dear to Edwin, going back against
the flow of Time in defiance of the "astronomic world", to see "the dead
world grow green within / Imagination's one long day"' (*B* 146). In the

later autobiographical article 'Yesterday's Mirror', Muir himself was to describe the search for self-knowledge in similar terms:

> what we require for real self-knowledge is the power to stop the sun and make it revolve in the opposite direction, taking us back stage by stage through manhood to youth and through youth to childhood, missing nothing, until it conducts us to the mystery from which we started.

While the mature Muir acknowledged that to attain such power was an impossibility, that 'at most we can take only a few chance leaps ᵦackward while Time hurries us on; and these fortuitous leaps we afterwards call our life',[15] the kind of exercise in which he indulges in 'The Stationary Journey' suggests an attempt to evade the circumstances of past and present actuality. Muir, like Keats in 'Ode to a Nightingale', has to learn that such indulgence is 'a dream' (*CP* 66).

As Peter Butter observes, 'most of the best poems in the volume are those in which the problems are dealt with obliquely through the experience of some historical or mythical character'.[16] In 'Merlin', for example, Muir achieves a fine blend of Arthurian legend and biblical myth in which to pursue the paradoxes of human mortality, the journeying backwards through time being here justified imaginatively by the legend of Merlin's magic powers.

Two poems, 'A Trojan Slave' and 'Troy', take their starting point from the legends of Greece. 'Troy' reworks the Platonic metaphor of our shadow world in its exploration of reality and illusion in human life in a context where arbitrary fate seems to dominate affairs. In this poem, an old man, left over from the battle for Troy, relives that battle as he fights the rats in the underground sewers of the city, and sees in these present foes the Greek heroes Ajax and Achilles. In his own heroic madness, he enacts not the destruction of Troy but his imagined conquering of the Greek warriors:

> And the wild Greeks yelled round him.
> Yet he withstood them, a brave, mad old man,
> And fought the rats for Troy.
>
> (*CP* 77)

Lillian Feder interprets Muir's use of Troy within the context of his Eden symbolism. She says:

> Troy appears frequently in Muir's poetry as the 'universal landscape' of man's inevitable fall from a happy and secure state. The protagonist of 'Troy' and the speaker of 'A Trojan Slave' are not unlike the questioner of 'The Fall' in that all look back to an

earlier period of legendary happiness. In 'The Fall', it is Eden that is the interior landscape; in 'Troy' and 'A Trojan Slave', the historical city has become a myth in man's memory. [17] While accepting the validity of this interpretation as one aspect of Muir's redevelopment of the Troy legends, one could argue that both these poems are more deeply pessimistic in the way that they act out through their mythical metaphor that obsession with determinism which is given form in Muir's early poetry in the imagery of restricted ways and our consequent lack of understanding and freedom. P. H. Gaskill comments that Muir and Hölderlin 'both seem to turn more naturally to Greece and the Middle East of the Bible than to the mythologies of their homelands'. [18] In Muir's case, the Scottish equivalent of a deterministic philosophy was Calvinism, with its doctrines of Original Sin and the Elect, and I believe that his turning to Greek myth is related to his philosophical battle with Calvinism, to his wish to reject that supposedly grace-ful but in reality, for many, grace-less form of religion and his simultaneous need to understand it and come to terms with it in the context of the events of his own early life. In the stories of Greece, as in Calvinist theology, an outcome is brought about not by the actions of human beings but by the will – often the arbitrary will – of the all-powerful gods. A hero's success in battle depends ultimately not on his own skill but on whether or not the gods decide to favour him. Oedipus in innocence treads a way which has been preordained a way of guilt. Penelope can only hope that the outcome of her actions will in the end justify her faith in a fate she cannot know or influence.

Muir's obsession with determinism may well have had its roots in his Orkney childhood. Although the strict form of Calvinism which had dominated the Scottish Kirk since the Reformation was on the wane in the late nineteenth century, such changes in belief are never clear-cut. In the middle of the century, both John McLeod Campbell, a minister of the Church of Scotland, and John Morison, of the United Secession Church, had been expelled for challenging the doctrines of Predestination and the Elect, and George Marshall recounts in *The Orkney Background of Edwin Muir* that among the 'live religious issues in the parish of Rousay' when Muir was a boy was 'the retention of Calvinist dogma in its strict form'. [19] Although Muir's family do not appear to have been strict Calvinists themselves or harsh in their moral attitudes, interest in theological disputation and an inclination to a literal interpretation of the Bible would appear to have been a family characteristic. Muir himself tells how speculation about the millennium 'sank deep into my mind, as I was to discover many years later' (*A* 28). Revivalist religious

meetings were also a feature of the time, and the effect of these on his
developing imagination is powerfully communicated in *An Autobiography*. In such a climate of contrasting religious practices and
disputes, it would be surprising if a child as sensitive to atmosphere as
Muir undoubtedly was did not absorb a sense of insecurity and obsession
with regard to religious beliefs. One childhood incident described in *An
Autobiography* which illustrates a deep-seated if illogical preoccupation
with sin and guilt and predestination is his account of a nervous crisis at
the age of seven when he was obsessed with guilt at having, possibly,
but without remembrance of the deed, touched the sheep dip which his
father had forbidden anyone to touch, and his endless washing of his
hands in the fruitless attempt to cleanse himself of that sin and its
repercussions (*A* 34).

From its earliest beginnings, then, Muir's work as critic and poet
exhibits this obsession with Calvinist theology. *We Moderns* contains
several aphorisms on Original Sin and the Fall and the restrictions
which a Calvinist view of existence places on human capacity for self-
determination and regeneration. As we have seen, the motif of the
restricted way is a recurring one in the early poetry. For Willa Muir,
reflecting on her husband's preoccupation with themes of the Fall and
Original Sin, 'so irrational an obsession . . . must have taken root in his
unconscious at an early, very impressionable age' (*B* 249).

In his employment of the legends of Greece, Muir modifies the myths
to suit the shifting nature of his search, acting out different scenarios as
he explores human constriction in various forms and with varying
outcomes. While 'A Trojan Slave', for example, could be interpreted
from an imperialist or class perspective, the slaves being considered a
subject race or too inferior a class to be entrusted with the defence of
Troy, one could also interpret the poem in the context of Calvinist
theology. The seeds of the destruction of Troy would appear to have lain
within Troy itself like some form of Original Sin. No matter what
heroic feats were enacted by the Trojan warriors, the battle could not be
won while they were irrevocably weakened by the nature of a society
where membership of the 'Elect' could not be extended. The slaves, the
rejected ones, could not be allowed to fight for Troy.

In the poem 'Troy', the scenario is also a negative one. However
attractive it might be to interpret the poem optimistically as the story of
an old man holding faith with an ideal in spite of the chaos around him,
one has to acknowledge that the old man's faithfulness is negated by his
madness. Just as in 'The Other Oedipus' from *One Foot in Eden* Oedipus
escapes from the horror of his innocent sin and punishment into the

'storyless' world of madness, so the old man in this poem does not realise – cannot realise – that his faithfulness is to unreality, to the shadow world. Even while he fights the imaginary Greeks, Muir tells us that 'mysterious shadows fell / Affrighting him whenever a cloud offended / The sun up in the other world' (*CP* 77): an ominous reminder that power remains elsewhere. Then arbitrary fate takes a hand. Some robbers by chance come upon him and think he must be hunting for the lost treasure of Troy. He is brought from the illusion of his shadow world in the sewers to the cruel reality of the world above. His mad dream is shattered, he is tortured for the non-existent treasure and dies. In this poem, the possibility of human choice and positive action would appear to be negated, both by the madness of the old man which keeps him in the world of illusion as opposed to reality, and by the chance, arbitrary operations of Fate through its instruments, the equally-deluded robbers. There would appear to be no way forward for humanity in such a fickle, meaningless world.

Madness is again an aspect of the poems 'Tristram's Journey' and 'Hölderlin's Journey'. 'Hölderlin's Journey' is a compelling, provocative poem, but, as in much of Muir's early poetry, there is an ambiguity in the working-out of theme and imagery which appears to be unintentional, as opposed to the creative use of ambiguity which is to be found in his later work. Here he takes as framework the biographical details of Hölderlin's love for his Diotima (Susette Gontard), his enforced parting from her, the return journey which finds her dead, and his final madness, and by telescoping these events in time produces a poem which is tense, dramatic and causally constructed. 'Hölderlin's Journey' has been variously interpreted by critics. Elizabeth Huberman sees a positive outcome in Hölderlin's recognition of the truth of Diotima's death and reconciliation in the poem's final lines as, despite his 'broken mind', he is found 'giving thanks to God and man'.[20] P. H. Gaskill, on the other hand, questions such an optimistic interpretation and points to the implications of Hölderlin's madness. Whatever insights Hölderlin may have gained through his suffering, these cannot be meaningfully related to human life because of his madness. The ending of the poem is therefore in his view less a true reconciliation of suffering with understanding and acceptance than the 'praising . . . of an idiot'.[21] The poem is thus close to the 'Troy' poem, both in the presentation of madness as a dominant feature of its principal character and in the ambiguity of interpretation to which this leads. In addition, Hölderlin, in Muir's scenario, suffers from the unknown predestined fate which afflicts so many of the characters in Muir's poems:

> 'For now I know
> Diotima was dead . . .
>
> 'Before I left the starting place;
> Empty the course, the garland gone . . .'
>   (*CP* 74)

Once again we are faced with the futility of human action in a world
where outcomes are determined in a context outwith our influence, and
once again we find Muir devising evasive scenarios in the attempt to
counteract this. What we have in this poem, it seems to me, is not the
divine madness of a prophet/poet, but a final madness which is the
consequence of a fate too severe to be borne, the 'dragging in pain' of 'a
broken mind' (*CP* 74) which Muir himself had perhaps feared in his
early years.

The poem which is perhaps a paradigm for Muir's antithetical,
ambivalent searching in these early poems is 'The Mythical Journey', in
which, as in 'The Hill', he again turns to the north/south opposition as a
metaphor for the nature of the human journey and its wished-for but
uncertain end:

> First in the North. The black sea-tangle beaches,
> Brine-bitter stillness, tablet-strewn morass,
> Tall women against the sky with heads covered,
> The witch's house below the black-toothed mountain,
> Wave-echo in the roofless chapel,
> The twice-dead castle on the swamp-green mound,
> Darkness at noon-day, wheel of fire at midnight,
> The level sun and the wild shooting shadows.
>   (*CP* 69)

There are no finite verbs in this first verse paragraph. Instead we have a
piling-up of compound adjectives and adjectival phrases which evoke
the dark, unyielding, static condition of life in the unwanted north.
The second verse opens with a question which implies change: 'How
long ago?' From there, movement is begun through participles and
participial adjectives – 'sailing up', 'rivers of running gold' – to the
positive finite action of 'the ship hastened on and brought him to / The
towering walls of life and the great kingdom'. The imagery of 'gold',
'sun' and 'summer isles' suggests that this is the longed-for south, the
place of 'pattern' and 'meaning' (*CP* 70). Yet in the end, this poem, too,
reaches 'a conclusion without fulfilment'. In his vision, the poet sees, as
did Hölderlin in 'Hyperions Schiksaalslied', 'the gods [who] reclined
and conversed with each other / From summit to summit'. There is not

in Muir, however, the certainty of the German poet's vision. As in 'The Lost Land' from *First Poems*, the light is 'wavering', the meaning caught for 'a moment', then 'as he looked, nothing / Was there but lights and shadows'. The vision of the gods on their hill is surrounded by dreamlike, ambiguous imagery – 'plain of glass', 'crystal grave' and

> all the dead scattered
> Like fallen stars, clustered like leaves hanging
> From the sad boughs of the mountainous tree of Adam
> Planted far down in Eden.
>
> (*CP* 70)

However seductive poetically, this imagery has the effect of unsettling the positive vision of the gods which would appear to have been the goal of the poem. In the end, the speaker can only build 'in faith and doubt his shaking house' (*CP* 70). In this phrase, one notices an influence from Hölderlin which will become a characteristic feature of Muir's own style: the use of the unifying conjunction 'and' to link two apparent irreconcilables. Here, this has the effect of highlighting the unresolved state of the search at this point in time while pointing also to the fact that these seeming polarities are somehow both inexplicably involved in its fulfilment: an intuition which was to remain an essential part of his philosophical journey in his poetry.

NOTES

1. Philip Mairet, quoted by Philip Conford in 'Unsung Hero of an Ephemeral Art', *Times Higher Education Supplement*, 16 November 1984, p. 15.
2. Edwin Muir, 'A Note on the Scottish Ballads', *Freeman* VI, 17 January 1923, pp. 441–4. Collected in *Latitudes* (London: Melrose, 1924), p. 15 and *Edwin Muir: Uncollected Scottish Criticism*, ed. A. Noble (London: Vision Press, 1982), pp. 156–7.
3. See Muir's essay 'North and South', *Latitudes*, pp. 103–14.
4. Johann Wolfgang von Goethe, 'Kennst du das Land?', *The Harrap Anthology of German Poetry*, ed. August Closs and T. Pugh Williams (London: Harrap, 1957), pp. 219–20.
5. Goethe, *Harrap Anthology*, p. 220.
6. Edwin Muir, 'A Question to my Love', *New Age* XIV, no 7, 18 December 1913, p. 197.
7. Hugo von Hofmannsthal, 'Ballade des äusseren Lebens', *Harrap Anthology*, p. 493.
8. Friedrich Hölderlin, 'Da ich ein Knabe war', *Harrap Anthology*, p. 272.
9. George Marshall, *In a Distant Isle: The Orkney Background of Edwin Muir* (Edinburgh: Scottish Academic Press, 1987), p. 140.

10. Rainer Maria Rilke, 'Das ist die Sehnsucht', *Harrap Anthology*, p. 498.

11. See P. H. Gaskill, 'Edwin Muir in Hellerau', *Scottish Literary Journal* no 11, May 1984, pp. 45–6.

12. T. S. Eliot, 'Burnt Norton', *Four Quartets*, Faber paperback ed. (London: Faber & Faber, 1959), p. 17.

13. Heinrich Heine, *Harrap Anthology*, p. 52.

14. Friedrich Hölderlin, *Harrap Anthology*, p. 273.

15. Edwin Muir, 'Yesterday's Mirror', *Scots Magazine* XXXIII, no 6, September 1940, p. 404.

16. Peter Butter, *Edwin Muir: Man and Poet* (Edinburgh and London: Oliver & Boyd, 1966), p. 142.

17. Lillian Feder, *Ancient Myth in Modern Poetry* (Princeton: Princeton University Press, 1971), p. 372.

18. P. H. Gaskill, 'Hölderlin and the Poetry of Edwin Muir', *Forum for Modern Language Studies* 16, 1980, p. 30.

19. T. C. Smout, *A Century of the Scottish People 1830–1950* (London: Collins, 1986), Fontana paperback ed. (1987), pp. 192–3. Marshall, *The Orkney Background of Edwin Muir*, p. 109.

20. Elizabeth Huberman, *The Poetry of Edwin Muir: The Field of Good and Ill* (New York: Oxford University Press, 1971), p. 93.

21. Gaskill, 'Hölderlin and the Poetry of Edwin Muir', p. 14.

Two

Autobiography and the Novel

The Muirs spent a year in France in 1926–7, living first of all in St Tropez and then in Menton. Their principal occupation was the translation of Feuchtwanger's *Jud Süss* for the American publisher Huebsch, but both had in addition plans to write novels of their own. Muir wrote to Sydney Schiff from St Tropez in May 1926:

> My novel is becoming more clear every day; though I think there may be quite a struggle when I sit down to it. We have being doing prodigies in translation. Only 24 pages remain now out of the 610, and when they are done we are going to take a week's holiday before we sit down to our novels. (*SL* 55–6)

Willa Muir's projected novel was *Imagined Corners*, published in 1931, and Edwin's *The Marionette* (1927).

It is perhaps not surprising that Muir turned to the novel at this time. Since the early 1920s he had been active as a literary critic and reviewer, and his most recent collection of critical essays, *Transition* (1926), had to a significant extent been concerned with the fiction of Joyce, Lawrence, Woolf and Huxley, together with trends in contemporary fiction in general. The commission to translate Feuchtwanger's novel may also have awakened the desire to 'try' one for himself. In addition, his poetry-writing had run into difficulties. After the flow of poetry released by psychoanalysis and his first visit to Europe after his marriage, he seemed unable to find a suitable poetry medium for what he still needed to say. *Chorus of the Newly Dead*, although finding a sympathetic publisher in the Hogarth Press, remained 'a miscarried attempt', as Muir himself was to call it in a letter to Kathleen Raine many years later (*SL* 173). In the wake of the *Chorus*'s failure, it may be that prose fiction appeared to offer a more propitious medium through which suffering could be explored in a human yet impersonal way.

The Marionette, set in the Salzburg he had visited during his previous stay in Europe, has more in common with the imagination of Muir the poet than with the later novelist of *The Three Brothers* and *Poor Tom*. He described it to his publisher as 'less a novel than a sort of metaphysical or symbolical tragedy, and at the same time a perfectly straightforward tale' (*SL* 58). The reader is immediately struck by the relationship with Kafka, although Muir did not become acquainted with Kafka's writing until three years later. He wrote to Schiff in July 1929 that he had recently had the 'great good fortune' to come across Kafka's *Das Schloss*:

> Kafka's book is still more strange in its atmosphere; it is a purely metaphysical and mystical dramatic novel . . . everything happens on a mysterious spiritual plane which was obviously the supreme reality to the author; and yet in a curious way everything is given solidly and concretely.

He added: 'it appeals particularly to the part of me which wrote *The Marionette*' (*SL* 67).

The Marionette is written in a deceptively simple style, where words seem planted in the text with care, almost as if in translation. Sentences are on the whole short, simple in structure or with one subordinate clause only. Present participial phrases are frequent, as is the use of the conjunction 'and'. Colours are bright and sharply differentiated. This simple, direct style patterns the nature of the main character Hans, a mentally-deficient boy whose mother has died in giving birth to him. The stasis in his life, his enclosure in his own unworldly world, are recreated through the detailed, slow-moving pace of the first chapter where we encounter the boy's delight in empty rooms and silence, in the expanse of the long dining-table, in the flowers, tree and wall of the garden. 'The touch of inanimate things, of stone, moss, iron, or wood, made him feel secure' (*M* 7). On the other hand, movement unsettled him: 'What moved could destroy, and all that moved some time did destroy' (*M* 11). In a passage which anticipates Muir's autobiography, we read that

> he saw nature as a terrifying heraldry. The cat, the lizard, and the wasp were embattled forces armed for war, carrying terror and death on their blazoned stripes, their stings, claws, and tongues. He could only run away from them to the vacancy of his room. (*M* 7–8)

At first, in grief, Hans's father rejects and ignores him, then, driven by pity when the servant Emma brings the boy formally to his study on his fourteenth birthday, he sets out to integrate him into life. The timelessness of the opening chapter is replaced by the sense of an action being set in motion which will proceed to its necessary end, whatever that may be; and, as in Kafka's novels, behind the directness and clarity of the narrative one is aware of a symbolic dimension as in fairytale or myth; a sense of the ultimate mystery of human life.

A reviewer of the 1987 paperback reprint of *The Marionette* described Muir as 'one of the last, and greatest, European traditionalists',[1] and it is this quality of European imagination rather than the influence of English or Scottish fiction which dominates the novel. Alongside the sense of transcendent mystery to which he responded in Kafka and Hölderlin lies the expressionism and grotesquerie of German and Austrian culture as found in much poetry and painting, in the fairytales of Grimm, in Salzburg itself with its twisting streets and puppet theatre and the Stations of the Cross on the way up to the Kapuzinerberg, and in the strange Christmas rituals of the Krampus demons described by Willa Muir in *Belonging*. More sinisterly, behind the fears of Hans, the name-calling and stone-throwing of local boys and Hans's own crucifixion of the marionette Gretchen is the shadow of *Der Eiserne Besen* (A 214) with its persecution of the Jews, and an anticipation of the persecution which was to come.

The Marionette, then, is a novel which works on more than one level and with various possible interpretations. At its most simple, it is the story of Hans and his father who, separated through death, illness and grief, come together to make a new life with each other through involvement with the marionette theatre. At another level, Hans is the child in all of us, who has to learn to move from the safety of home and absorption with self into the external world of alien forces and challenging identities, a world with which he must come to terms if he is to achieve an integrated personality. Muir, rereading the novel twenty years after its first publication, found that while it did not tell him much that he had forgotten about Salzburg, it did tell him 'a great deal about the mingled excitement and fear which we feel on setting foot in a town we have never seen before'. For him, Salzburg is seen through Hans's eyes 'with the simplicity of one who does not understand what he sees . . . the first impressions of a child come new into the midst of new things' (A 215). *The Marionette* is also a story about illusion and reality in our daily world and a metaphysical tale of preordained action and deceptive freedom, where wisdom is, as in many traditional tales, achieved through the insight of the simple-minded. Although one would not want to foreground an autobiographical interpretation at the expense of its rich plurality of meaning, as Muir's autobiographical comment hints, it is also, perhaps unconsciously, a part of his ongoing exploration of his own lost past and his attempt to bring together his present being and the lost land of his childhood. At this level of interpretation, it is possible to see father and son as the adult Muir and his lost child's self, and the father's attempt to bring Hans into the real world through an involvement with the fictional

world of the marionettes as the adult Muir's attempt to make contact
through his creative writing with the childhood world *re*-presented to
him through his dreams and memories', and thus to integrate past and
present in a new wholeness.

Muir's ending is entirely in keeping with all levels of interpretation
and with the material facts of his story. There is no miraculous cure for
Hans. Nevertheless, after two traumatic episodes in which the
accidental breaking of the marionette Gretchen and the persecution of
local boys lead him to a realisation of the artificiality and fictional nature
of his marionette world, he is eventually enabled to enter into his
father's and our world and, although still disabled, work successfully
and with peace and happiness as his father's gardener. The sudden
transition from past to present tense in the final paragraph underlines
both the completion of the process of the narrative and the point of
equilibrium that Hans has reached. He will continue as he is, but this
new present or timelessness is no longer one of paralysis, but an
involvement in the living moments of the garden which he tends. The
father, too, has accepted the present and no longer rejects or attempts to
change Hans. Indeed, 'through long association father and son have
come to resemble each other in their gestures and ways of speech'
(*M* 155). In a perceptive 'Afterword' to the 1987 reissue, Paul Binding
describes the novel as 'an account . . . of how – in Freudian terms –
Eros, the impulse to love, can win over Thanatos, the movement
towards death, without evading the latter's reality'.[2] This too is a
significant layer of meaning in the work, as is the recognition of the
restorative effect of play and artistic creativity, an insight deriving from
Jung, whose theories Muir found more sympathetic than those of Freud.

In July 1929, Muir was already writing that his second novel 'has
been in my head for over a year; none of it is written yet, however . . .
It will be in a completely different style from *The Marionette* – not at all
fantastic' (*SL* 67). So far as its surface subject matter is concerned, *The
Three Brothers* should belong to the historical novel genre. Set in the
Reformation period at the time of the killing of Cardinal Beaton of St
Andrews, it tells the story of the childhood of three brothers on their
father's farm, their adolescence as students in Reformation St Andrews
and their young adulthood and rivalry in the Edinburgh of Mary Queen
of Scots. On the other hand, Muir as critic was not enthusiastic about
the period and by implication the historical novel, commenting in *The
Structure of the Novel* that such works were 'a spurious kind of history
which occasionally breaks into fiction' (*SN* 123) and that they made
'everything particular, relative and historical' as opposed to showing us
'human truth valid for all time' (*SN* 117). His own novel is not

genuinely a historical novel, being much more concerned with the dramatic interplay of character and family relationships than it is with what Lukács has called the 'artistic demonstration of historical reality'.[3] In spite of the fact that Muir must have been writing his biography of John Knox (1929) while the novel was 'in his head', there is little vital sense of the impact which the Reformation made on the Scotland of the mid-sixteenth century. The Cardinal is murdered, the French fleet appears off the St Andrews coast, two brothers go off to fight for the Reformers while their mother is dying; but the focus is on the mother-son relationship, not on the historical events. Similarly, in the Edinburgh setting of the final part, one never has a sense of the Kirk-Court warfare of the period. Knox's fierce preaching is discussed, the Queen rides down the Royal Mile to Holyrood; but, if anything, the historical impression conveyed is that of the Edinburgh of Scott's *Heart of Midlothian* rather than that of the 1560s.

Muir's novel, then, cannot be truly categorised as a historical novel. On the other hand, it does conform to what Muir defined in *The Structure of the Novel* as the dramatic novel, being a novel of psychological relationships and depicting a journey towards self-knowledge and self-determination. Its three parts mark three important stages in the life of its principal character David, and the titles of these sections — 'David'; 'David and Archie'; 'David, Archie and Sandy' — show David moving from the establishment of his own identity in childhood into a situation of interpersonal peer relationships involving first two brothers, then all three.

One is tempted to a much greater extent than in *The Marionette* to interpret this novel as another stage in Muir's personal journey to understanding and integration. Its first section in particular records for the first time many of the incidents we have become familiar with through his later autobiography: the pig-sticking at the farm (here experienced by the twin brothers David and Archie) (*TB* 27–37); the fight with Freddie Flaws and the boy's legendary run home from school (*TB* 46–9); the wonder at the magnificence of the farm horses

> with their huge hulks sending out a glow in the darkness, the fire striking from the flags as they brought down their ponderous steel-shod hoofs, the clashing ring of the metal on the hard stone; all this sent a wild thrill to his heart as he stood in the doorway with the dying light in the yard behind him. (*TB* 57)

Even the libidinous Sutherland is there, and the father's exasperated comment: 'Why, the man canna look at them, it seems, without them getting in the family way!' (*TB* 26). The boy's troubled wonder at how the Cardinal could be killed in the centre of his many-roomed and well-guarded castle, and the father's explanation concerning the gate, 'a wee thing that ye would hardly notice, a wee, wicked-looking, wee gate' (*TB* 12), look forward to Muir's later *Narrow Place* poem on the same subject.

Part I is the most successful of the novel's three parts, and it succeeds despite its lack of historical focus because of the essential timelessness of the young child's world and the relative timelessness of a farm's cycle of work patterns. Here are the first intimations of that idealised vision of childhood which was to be created so powerfully in Muir's later autobiography. Although the story line accommodates twin brothers, as opposed to the perspective of the single child in the autobiography, it is the questioning, sensitive child, suggestive of the later self-portrait, with whom the narrative is principally concerned, not the quick-tongued, gregarious and self-confident twin. As in *The Marionette*, the father is the one who leads the boy out of his isolation into a degree of self-confidence and independence, while in this novel the mother's obvious preference for his twin saps his self-esteem. The first part ends with David's acquisition of the (mother-forbidden) skill of swimming and a new faith in his own powers.

Muir wrote to his sister Lizzie about his third novel, *Poor Tom*, that she should not 'look for any living model (or dead one either) for any of the characters: that would be completely wrong, for they are all synthetic, made up of scraps taken from all sorts of nooks and corners, and mostly pure imagination, like the main situation' (*SL* 78). To a degree, all good novels are autobiographical since their success depends on their author's capacity to enter imaginatively into the scenarios which he or she creates and to draw upon previous emotional experience in order to bring them alive for the reader. Yet, despite Muir's disclaimer, one senses that *Poor Tom* and *The Three Brothers* may be autobiographical in a more specific way and that they are reworking and reinterpreting emotional crises from his past. In both novels, one meets very similar scenarios of sibling rivalry and betrayal, including sexual betrayal, which, when taken with the considerable amount of recognisable biographical background in the books, leads one to suspect that Muir's family and young adult relationships were not entirely free from competition and aggression.

Betrayal is a principal theme in Parts II and III of the novel. In the second part, David has to come to terms with the fact that Archie will put aside loyalty to his brother and his dying mother if his own perceived needs are more pressing. He has to watch his brother exulting in his role as hero as a result of his exploits with the Protestant Reformers, while he himself is cast even lower in his fellow students' eyes by virtue of his having fetched a Catholic priest to his mother. As in their childhood days, Archie does not try to defend his brother from the students' taunts and threatened violence, and David suspects that Archie may be the one who has made known his association with the priest. In the third part, Archie's betrayal is sexual as he takes over David's girl and makes her pregnant, thus contributing to her violent death at the hands of a former outraged suitor. Self-interest is everywhere in this portrayal of Calvinist Edinburgh, a setting which shares many of the mores of the Glasgow of Muir's youth. Here, also, we meet the red-haired, violent woman of *An Autobiography*, with her cries of 'It's him that put me on the streets', and the two fighting men: 'I ken he's done me no harm, but I'm going to do him harm' (*TB* 196). Like the street fighter, Sandy and Archie's new-found Calvinism teaches them to do harm to others lest it is done to them, and has led Sandy to a cynicism which sees ugliness and deceit everywhere:

> the sight o' goodness fills ye wi' a scunner, for you ken it's no' what it seems − it canna be; but the pleasure's [in seeing evil in folk] a gey queer kind of pleasure too, you would be better without it. Folk are no better than beasts, Davie, when you see them in their right colours. (*TB* 203)

Sandy's experience parallels Muir's account of the evils of Calvinism in his hostile biography of Knox. He wrote to Schiff in a letter accompanying a copy of the biography that

> it was more particularly written for the purpose of making some breach in the enormous reverence in which Knox has been held and is still held in Scotland, a reverence which I had to fight with too in my early days (so that I really feel quite strongly about it) and which has done and is doing a great deal of harm. It is astonishing (and has given me a great distrust of biographies) that all the worst utterances and doings of Knox which I have mentioned have all been quietly suppressed by his former biographers. (*SL* 66)

Set in this Calvinist context, the third section of the novel is much taken up with the 'why' of human existence: why do things happen in life as they do? Why do human beings act towards each other as they do? Why should one person be spared and another have to die? Sandy's anguish is quenched only at the point of death when he rejects Calvinism and sends for an Anabaptist preacher to comfort him. The novel ends with David's vision of Judgment Day with its command to 'Choose, choose' (a vision transformed into poetry in the late poem 'The Last Judgment'); with his return to his father's farm and his eventual setting-forth to travel in England and Holland. ' "You've all the world before you", said his father. "You're bound to find some vocation somewhere in it to suit you"' (*TB* 343). Ironically, then, Muir's second novel ends in exactly the same way that he had condemned so often as reviewer of contemporary fiction. It is, as many contemporary novels were, a novel without an ending, and a novel without an ending, according to Muir the critic, shows an inadequate philosophy of life. Like David, Muir himself would appear still to be searching for a way forward.

The Three Brothers was not a critical success: 'a pretty complete failure publicly, and there's little more to be said about it', as Muir wrote shortly after its publication in 1931 (*SL* 69). *Poor Tom* , which followed it in the space of a year, was not a success either. Muir wrote to the painter William Johnstone, who designed the book jacket, that his design was 'a brilliant piece of work, full of imagination and power, and extraordinarily ingenious in its use of the various motives in the book, of which you make something quite original'. The book, however, according to Johnstone, sold only about eighty copies (*SL* 77).

Despite this lack of public acclaim, *Poor Tom* , Muir's last attempt at the novel, is stylistically not a bad book. In addition, it has a not inconsiderable place as a historical portrait of young, emergent, working-class men in the early years of this century, while it continues the autobiographical exploration of *The Three Brothers* , bringing fiction and life into closer alignment with its setting in pre-1914 Glasgow.

Poor Tom is the kind of autobiographical novel categorised in *The Structure of the Novel* as a contemporary variation on the chronicle novel and exemplified in works such as Lawrence's *Sons and Lovers* , Joyce's *A Portrait of the Artist as a Young Man* and Bennett's *Clayhanger* trilogy. To these one might add Somerset Maugham's *Of Human Bondage* and, to take an example by a female author, *Open the Door!* by the Scottish writer Catherine Carswell. In all these works, the thinly-disguised author/ protagonist works through a process of throwing off the restraints imposed by family, education, religion and/or provincial culture to achieve a new self-understanding and self-determination. Maugham's 'Foreword' to *Of Human Bondage* could be seen to speak equally for *Poor Tom*. For Maugham, his novel

> is not an autobiography, but an autobiographical novel; fact and fiction are inextricably mingled; the emotions are my own, but not all the incidents are related as they happened and some of them are transferred to my hero not from my own life but from that of persons with whom I was intimate. The book did for me what I wanted and when it was issued to the world . . . I found myself free from the pains and unhappy recollections that had tormented me.[4]

Poor Tom's hero is Mansie Manson, a young man trying to find a way
forward to manhood through the new cultural activities opening up to
young working-class men at the turn of the century. There are vestiges
of Samuel Smiles's 'Self-Help' preaching in these activities as there were
in Muir's own youthful pursuits. Mansie, like Muir, joins the Clarion
Scouts, an organisation associated with the socialist newspaper *The
Clarion* . However, unlike the hero of Neil M. Gunn's turn-of-the-
century novel, *The Serpent*, who embraces socialism joyfully as an
ideology of freedom, Mansie's involvement is uncertain, even embarrassed.
On the other hand, and as in Gunn's novel also, what comes over
strongly in the novel is the *fear* of socialism among the respectable
working class; an association of socialism with atheism and a horror of
both which seems stronger than awareness of the need to alleviate the
degradation of the poorest in society. In the area of lighter leisure
pursuits, unlikely combinations are wrestling and dancing (with shiny
black dancing-pumps), together with rambling in the countryside
around Glasgow with young socialist companions. There are, in
addition, difficulties in relation to sexuality and the need to understand
and conform to respectable city mores in this area of activity.

Although at times the writing in the early chapters can be dull and
simultaneously rhetorical in a clichéd manner – 'some sheltered arbour
of this pleasance' (*PT* 30–1) – what is remarkable is its explicit account
of young male sexuality in the early years of the century. Muir's
communication of this may on occasions verge on the ludicrous, as in
his account of Mansie's seduction by the seemingly respectable Isa. He
is no prude, however, and treats sexuality as a normal part of human
activity. This is as it should be, but it is an attribute mostly lacking in
Scottish fiction by male authors, especially in the earlier decades of the
century. It is present, however, in early twentieth-century Scottish
female writers such as Catherine Carswell, Willa Muir and Naomi
Mitchison.

Nevertheless, while Muir's novel can be seen to relate to the genre of
autobiographical fiction, it is on the whole a more overtly philosophical
novel than any of those mentioned above. After an uncertain beginning,
when one is not clear whether the perspective is to be that of the
eponymous Tom or his brother Mansie, the novel coheres around the
relationship between Tom and Mansie, Tom's accident and Mansie's
attempts to come to terms with his feelings for his brother, Tom's
approaching death, the fact of mortality in general and the inexplicable
nature of human life itself. This makes for a very powerful narrative,
where the strength comes less from dramatic incident and variety in
characterisation than from the intensity with which the moral and

philosophical questions are posed and debated in Mansie's mind and imagination. While the novel stands on its own as a viable work of art and there is no need to go to Muir's life story for explanation or validation, one is nevertheless aware, if one knows that life story, how much Muir is drawing on the first shock of his experience of urban living in Glasgow and on the inexplicable tragedies which destroyed his family life and almost destroyed his own sanity. *Poor Tom* is therefore part of a philosophical continuum which embraces Muir's poetry, novels, criticism and autobiography, all of which, it seems to me, however independent and valid in their respective genres, are essentially motivated by and directed towards the need for understanding and philosophical equilibrium generated by the disruption and trauma of his early life. This does not make autobiographical interpretation an essential focus of Muir studies, but it does give his work as a whole an unusual thematic coherence over varied genres and over the span of a lifetime.

The philosophical heart of the novel is to be found in Chapters 16, 18 and 19, the period immediately after Tom's discharge from hospital and the beginning of his slow-motion fencing match with Time as the tumour on his brain gradually takes control of his body. 'All the life in the house seemed to slow down with the slowing down of Tom's bodily movements' (*PT* 155). Muir's narrative pace slows also, each detail of the sick man's movements painstakingly recorded and the circle of activity relentlessly closing into an essential preoccupation with life and death. Several of the memories later recorded in Muir's autobiography are here given to the dying Tom: the passing of the school playground with his mother as a small child and his smothering fear of the classroom as if he were to be 'shut in a clothes-cupboard' (*PT* 159); the young man on the farmer's cart in his northern home town, brought home to die. In two of these chapters, Muir uses epigraphs from Rilke and Nietzsche which give expression to the sense of alienation, the hopelessness and desperate search for some meaning in life which is experienced principally by Mansie, but also to some degree by all the family, including Tom himself. As in the epigraph from Rilke, contact with the animal world crystallises Mansie's awareness of his disconnectedness in a world he had previously taken for granted. Having taken advantage of the Glasgow autumn holiday weekend to escape into the countryside around the city, he comes across a young horse at a gate in a field and finds himself unable to pass through. This moment of apprehension (in both senses of the word), of being taken, so to speak, out of time, patterns a remembered childhood experience with a horse, and brings with it a sudden intuition that Tom will not recover but will die. The experience is so irrational yet so intense that it unnerves him, making him dizzy and setting up a panic-stricken philosophical questioning in his mind as he eventually hurries on his way:

> It was outrageous to be pursued by such thoughts; besides they didn't seem to be his at all, they didn't seem real. They were like something you read about; why, maybe this was what people meant by poetry? And once more he felt relieved, for poetry wasn't real life; it was imagination. (*PT* 177–8)

Further on, he encounters one of his Clarion Scout friends, a scientist who has an explanation for all phenomena, including the disposition of the landscape. In an echo of *We Moderns* and an anticipation of Muir's later writing on the difference between the scientific and poetic imagination, Mansie finds that Geordie's scientific explanations about glaciation do not satisfy him: 'when it comes to the point, how did anything get where it is?' (*PT* 180). Here we have Muir's recurrent emphasis on 'the eternal problem' as opposed to the problems of everyday life. Mansie, however, has to cope both with the problems of everyday life in regard to his brother's imminent death and with the philosophical mystery of life and death itself.

Mansie is not presented in the novel as an especially perceptive or intellectual character, and Muir accordingly keeps his questionings in an appropriate register, but the sense of terror at the sudden loss of acceptance of one's human and natural environment is no less forcibly communicated. His Cartesian debate with himself is put forward in the kind of agitated, basic questionings which might be forced out of any one of us by sudden, unexpected disaster, when the world as we have known it takes on an alien, incomprehensible identity. Chapter 19 takes as epigraph Nietzsche's 'Warum? Wofür? Wodurch? Wohin? Wo? Wie?' and so continues the meditation of the previous chapter. Muir abstracts this chapter from the linear pattern of the novel, putting it entirely into the hands of an anonymous speaker. Formally, this provides a space in the action which helps convey the waiting, the period of arrested time in the process of Tom's illness. Philosophically, it allows Muir to put Mansie's speculations into the voice of a more educated and mature observer and so bring out more clearly the issues troubling him and his author. Again, as in the Edinburgh section of *The Three Brothers* and in the criticism of the values of the modern age in *We Moderns* , the issue is the conflict between the 'how' of this world's activities as opposed to the eternal 'why', the secular preoccupation with the nuts and bolts of society as opposed to the religious concern with ultimate meaning and values. For Muir and his narrator, 'this How, this pseudo-Why' can provide only 'shifting ground beneath one's feet'

(*PT* 190) as even the socialist dream is in the end invalidated by the fact of mortality. For there is no place for death in the optimistic, evolutionary socialist creed, something which Mansie finds out through the inadequacy of his socialist friends in the face of Tom's mortal illness.

As with *The Three Brothers*, *Poor Tom* ends in the open way so often condemned by Muir the reviewer. Tom's illness and death have forced his brother to review his relationships and ideological affiliations, but he has not yet found a new way forward. In addition, it has brought forth the realisation of the 'provisional circle of life' (*PT* 252), its inevitable imperfection. In life, Tom and Mansie could not achieve the perfect friendship that each in his heart longed for: their sibling rivalry stood in the way. In death, when it is now too late, Mansie feels he perceives the individual nature of his brother as he had not previously been able to do. Inevitably, one is led to make associations with Muir's late poem 'The Brothers', in which the speaker, like Mansie, perceives his brothers transfigured, the old rivalries and enmities dissolved. The novel ends with the anticipation of Tom's funeral and with Mansie hastening to make a fresh start, freed from the life-denying ideologies which he has previously pursued.

The reappearance in Muir's autobiography of many of the incidents and memories narrated in *Poor Tom* and *The Three Brothers* raises the question of just how reliable Muir's autobiography is as an account of his childhood and adolescence. If autobiography has become the matter of fiction in the autobiographical novel, then how certain can we be that fiction has not in the end entered into the remembering and representing of the life story itself? In his 1987 book *In a Distant Isle: The Orkney Background of Edwin Muir*, George Marshall points to discrepancies between Muir's account of the Wyre of his childhood and what the Orkney Archives actually have to offer as evidence for social conditions at that time. In opposition to Muir's idealisation of Wyre and his observation that the island was remote enough for life to have remained almost unchanged for two hundred years, Marshall demonstrates that Wyre, like many of the Orkney parishes, was in the midst of an economic and social upheaval in the second half of the nineteenth century. The Orkney Roads Act of 1857 introduced roads and carts to the islands, and the first road on Wyre was made in 1893 during Muir's childhood there – an event which Marshall suggests may have been responsible for the adult Muir's obsession with the road as symbol in his poetry. The estate of Rousay, of which the smaller Wyre was part, was in the forefront of the 'improvement' movement. Here, the inhabitants were cleared from their farms, not to make way for sheep as in the Clearances of mainland Highland communities, but so that fencing and draining could be carried out and larger, more profitable farms created. With the impulse towards profitable farms came a money economy previously unknown in the islands, and with it the fear of economic failure and a change in traditional community relationships. Muir's family were initially beneficiaries of the changes, since these allowed them as incomers to rent the biggest and best farm on Wyre. In the end, however, their inability to pay the high rent demanded by their landlord forced them to move to a less good farm on Wyre, then to a poor farm on Mainland island, and finally to give up farming altogether with the subsequent ill-advised move to Glasgow. As Marshall suggests, it would seem that Muir's 'memories' of the tranquillity, harmony and timelessness of Wyre are more relevant to the world of his father's boyhood than to his own.[5]

Muir's autobiography *The Story and the Fable* and its revised and enlarged form *An Autobiography* are powerful documents, but it is perhaps naive to expect that autobiographical writing should be synonymous with the life lived. In *The Structure of the Novel*, Muir is in no doubt that one cannot equate art directly with life. Each has its own pattern, and the pattern of art is not the same as that of life. Similarly, a formal autobiography (as opposed to immediate diary jottings – although even these may be selective and subjective) has its own aesthetic pattern imposed by the necessary selection and ordering of remembered material, and in Muir's case this selection, ordering and communication of memories had already consciously taken place on at least two occasions in the writing of his second and third novels and, perhaps more unconsciously, in the writing of several of the poems in *First Poems* and during composition of *The Marionette*, with its focus on the child's uncomprehending view of the world. Muir himself set great store by the faculty of memory, seeing it as one with the 'articulate breath' which distinguishes us from the unmemoried world of the animals and as the essential link between past and present which gives our lives meaning and fulfilment. It may be truer to experience, however, to observe, as Catherine Carswell did in the 'Author's Note' to her unfinished autobiography: 'To be bound for ever by the arbitrary, accident of one's memories: what an idea of immortality!'[6] If, for most of us, our memories represented the totality of the life lived, then that life would have been a partial one indeed. In the essay 'Yesterday's Mirror', written after the publication of *The Story and the Fable*, Muir wrote that 'now that my autobiography was finished, I could really write my autobiography'[7] – a comment that hints at autobiographical *composition* and re-creation as opposed to a more straightforward remembering. One could perhaps say with some justification that once

Muir had written his autobiographical novels, he was in a position to compose his autobiography.

I would therefore see Muir's autobiographical writings as part of his wider discourse about the nature of human life, about an idealised vision of what that life might be and the reality to which we all have to accommodate ourselves. His autobiography itself should not be regarded in terms of how true or misremembered it is, but should be seen as part of the philosophical discourse conducted in his work as a whole and as part of the wider Romantic discourse. Conversely, it is important to recognise the autobiographical dimension in his early poetry and in his fiction, because it was this reworking of the memories and traumas of his childhood and young adulthood which freed his imagination for the mature poetry from *The Narrow Place* onwards. Muir's late imagery validates itself aesthetically and philosophically without the need for autobiographical intervention, while his subject matter becomes both increasingly topical and more widely relevant. It was, however, that unusual and traumatic life experience which enabled him to evoke so powerfully the chaos of war-torn Europe and the search for a philosophy which would take account of the contrary states of the human soul.

NOTES

1. J. Bamforth, Review of reprint of Edwin Muir, *The Marionette*, *Times Literary Supplement*, 4 March 1988, p. 253.
2. Paul Binding, 'Afterword' to reprint of *The Marionette* (1927) (London: Hogarth Press, 1987), penultimate page.
3. Georg Lukács, *The Historical Novel* (London: Merlin Press, 1962), p. 43.
4. W. Somerset Maugham, 'Foreword' to *Of Human Bondage* (1915) (London: Mandarin Paperbacks, 1990), p. 3.
5. Marshall, *The Orkney Background of Edwin Muir*, p. 86.
6. Catherine Carswell, 'Author's Note' to *Lying Awake: An Unfinished Autobiography and Other Posthumous Papers*, ed. with an introduction by John Carswell (London: Secker & Warburg, 1950).
7. Edwin Muir, 'Yesterday's Mirror', *Scots Magazine* XXXIII, p. 404.

Three

The Single, Disunited World

I

The Narrow Place and *The Voyage*

'His work . . . has caught a flame – from the fire that is burning the world.' These were the terms in which the novelist Neil M. Gunn reviewed Muir's collection *The Narrow Place* in the *Scots Magazine* of May 1943. For Gunn, Muir's previous work had 'at its best . . . always been spare and austere. . . . Yet occasionally one had the strange feeling that Muir could not get life's sure outline until years of death had fixed it permanently.' Now, however, he 'frequently deals with life in its living moment in the world of to-day, without any loss in strength of outline, in concentration, or in power'.[1]

Gunn is the Scottish writer with whom Muir has most affinity. Both spent their childhood in the 'northland', in simple, communal and cooperative communities, and both shared a sense of the importance of that way of life which was fast disappearing under the pressures of the modern world. Although both were also essentially philosophical writers, Gunn from the first was concerned to deal with the matter of today in his Highland novels, however uncomfortable this might be, and not to engage, as he said of Sir Walter Scott, in a 'story-telling or romance' which 'had interpretative bearing neither upon a present nor a future'.[2] Gunn was therefore well placed to appreciate the new direction that Muir's work had taken, and his comments catch the vital tone of *The Narrow Place*.

This new direction is given voice immediately in the first poem of the collection. 'To J. F. H. (1897–1934)' was written in memory of Muir's friend, John Holms, who died at a relatively early age without having in any concrete way fulfilled the potential his friends had perceived in him, and who was suddenly brought back into Muir's mind by the chance sighting of a motorcyclist who physically resembled him. The mixed sporting metaphors with which the poem opens pattern the shock of the

encounter and the reckless vitality which Muir had admired in his
friend:

> Shot from the sling into the perilous road,
> The hundred mile long hurtling bowling alley,
> To-day I saw you pass full tilt for the jack.
>
> (*CP* 95)

The imagery is immediate in a topical way new to Muir's work —
'trussed to the motor cycle'; 'the tension of your face'; 'the hot still
afternoon'. Yet the poem is able also to contain his characteristic
preoccupation with time eternal behind time present:

> I could not tell
> For a moment in the hot still afternoon
> What world I walked in, since it held us two,
> A dead and a living man.
>
> (*CP* 95)

In addition to the immediacy and everyday quality in the imagery, one
notices a more assured conversational verse movement, where the lines
with their irregular rhyming patterns move confidently towards a stress
on significant words and phrases, or towards that pregnant silent beat
which would become a feature of the formal organisation of poems in
which Muir depicted a moment out of time:

> The clock-hand moved, the street slipped into its place,
> Two cars went by.
>
> (*CP* 96)

Most commentators are agreed on the new-found maturity of *The
Narrow Place*, and there has also been considerable consensus as to the
reason for this. From this point onwards, one increasingly finds Muir's
achievement as a poet being discussed in the context of the deepening of
his spiritual life. The event in his religious experience which is most
often singled out as the harbinger of his poetic advance is his realisation
in February 1939, as he found himself reciting the Lord's Prayer in a
time of great personal distress, that he was a Christian. For Peter
Butter, 'the considerable advance poetically between *Journeys and Places*
(1937) and *The Narrow Place* (1943) was related to, and in part caused
by, this deepening of his spiritual life'.[3] Elizabeth Huberman ties
Muir's poetry more closely to religious interpretation and sees *The
Narrow Place* as the collection in which he finally resolves the dilemma
of 'whether to choose the darker or the brighter view' of human
existence. For her, 'The Gate' at the midpoint of the volume is 'the

nadir of horror and desolation', after which the way is upwards to 'a
rebirth into the light of acceptance and praise'.[4]

While not wishing to devalue the influence of Christianity on Muir's
poetry, I believe that critics have on the whole been too ready to see
transcendence as the goal and achievement of his work and to interpret
it in a predominantly Christian context. Willa Muir, too, was hesitant
about such focus on the Christian dimension, writing to Ernest and
Janette Marwick in November 1966 about Peter Butter's study of Muir
that 'he over-emphasises the religious motifs that matter more to him
than the poetry'.[5] What is evident from the poetry itself is that Muir's
involvement with religion is a search for meaning — what he described
in *An Autobiography* as 'where we came from, where we are going, and,
since we are not alone, but members of a countless family, how we
should live with one another' (*A* 56). His most effective poetry stems
from his response to mundane experience and his attempt to understand
and order it, not from the attempt to transcend it through the
imposition of a Christian solution. Nor does the realisation of his
personal Christian belief seem an adequate explanation of his new-found
stylistic maturity.

Perhaps the philosophical significance of the 1939 experience lies in
Muir's realisation of the universality of the Lord's Prayer, of its relevance
to the here and now: 'I never realised before so clearly the primary
importance of "we" and "us" in the prayer: it is collective, for all
societies, for all mankind as a great society'.[6] This insight related to
other circumstances of his life at that time which were conspiring to
bring the everyday world into his poetry. In 1935, as a result of an
accident to their young son, the Muirs had decided to leave Hampstead
for the quieter ambience of St Andrews in Scotland. This proved to be
an unfortunate move. After years spent in the intellectual ambience of
London and Europe, they found St Andrews narrow and provincial, and
Muir's London reputation as critic, poet and translator seemed to mean
little to the university community there. Scotland in general seemed to
be living up to the pessimistic accounts given in his reviews and books
in the early and mid-1930s. In addition, the war in Europe brought
financial problems as income from translating from German ceased.
Muir's efforts to obtain a teaching post in compensation proved to be a
sardonic parody of the Calvinist doctrine of the Elect which had so long
obsessed him, his entry to the heaven of teaching being entirely
dependent upon the certificate of the Elect which he did not possess. In
a letter to Alec Aitken of 12 June 1941, he tells how his

> lack of an academic degree is a most astonishing obstacle: in
> Scotland nothing but a certificate of some kind seems to be

recognised as really meritorious – a curious example of the
preference of faith to works, for surely by this time I've done some
work that should count. (*SL* 130)

The shock of his wife's illness which had provoked the unwitting
recourse to the Lord's Prayer was paralleled by his distress over the fate
of friends and acquaintances in war-torn Europe. Herman Broch himself
came as a refugee to their home in St Andrews. Later, Muir's contact
with the 'single, disunited world' of Europe was intensified when he
went to work with refugees and foreign servicemen in Edinburgh in the
early 1940s and when he witnessed in Prague in the immediate postwar
period the evils of the Nazi occupation of Czechoslovakia being replaced
by the authoritarianism of a communist regime.

As a consequence, it was no longer the personal tragedies and sense of
alienation from his own past which now obsessed him, but the problems
of the nightmare present in Europe with its implications for the fate of
all humanity. The poetry from *The Narrow Place* onwards increasingly
finds him able to use his personal experience as the springboard for a
leap into the condition of all humankind and so give voice to his sense of
our common fate, the legacy of his upbringing in the non-competitive,
cooperative community of the Orkney Isles.

In addition, Muir's long apprenticeship as a poet had at last provided
him with the tools with which to dissect his experience. He had become
skilled in the use of imaginative, pointed, descriptive language in prose
writings such as *Scottish Journey* and the first version of his autobiography, *The Story and the Fable*, not to speak of his fiction writing,
and it is this stylistic maturity which one now finds appearing in the
poetry also.

The Narrow Place and *The Voyage* are products of these immediate
prewar and war years. Both contain a mixture of philosophical, personal
and war-theme poems. 'The Wayside Station' of *The Narrow Place*,
which creates the context for the more overt war poems 'The River' and
'The Refugees' which follow, grew out of Muir's daily waiting at
Leuchars railway station for the train which would take him to his work
at the Dundee Food Office. The mood of despondency which it emits
would seem to be that of its poet as he contemplates the return to
futility in his daily life:

> Here at the wayside station, as many a morning,
> I watch the smoke torn from the fumy engine
> Crawling across the field in serpent sorrow.
> Flat in the east, held down by stolid clouds,
> The struggling day is born and shines already

On its warm hearth far off. Yet something here
Glimmers along the ground to show the seagulls
White on the furrows' black unturning waves.

(CP 96)

The slow, struggling into life of the cold east-coast morning is here depicted in a way which is both strongly visual and emotionally weighted. Words and images point to reluctant participation, meanness of response, dreary menace. All seems apathy and alienation. The smoke is 'torn' from the engine, while the alliteration in 'serpent sorrow' both echoes the hissing steam and draws attention to 'serpent' with its connotations of betrayal, a suggestion left undeveloped at this point. Clouds are 'stolid', indicative not only of the darkness persisting in the early-morning landscape but also of an inflexibility of response. The black, furrowed field may appear to be like the sea to the watching poet, but its waves are *un*turning, once again an image of arrestment.

This despondent mood continues in the second stanza as cattle and human beings take on the poet's reluctance to face the day. Only the bedroom seems to communicate an air of mystery and romance, but even it is now deserted by the young lovers and has become 'an inaccessible land'. In the last five lines, we find a change in the imagery which at first might seem to herald a more positive mood. We have individual words such as 'bright', 'silver'; active verbal phrases which point to change and movement such as the stream which 'leaps the gap of light' and 'starts its winding journey'; water, as in the stream image, is itself often a symbol for rebirth or a new beginning. These individual items are deceptive, however, and when related to the other images in the poem the 'message' continues to be a negative one. The light of dawn, as it increases, is seen not just as 'bright' but as a 'bright snare' which 'slips coil by coil' around the wood, as if imprisoning it. The stream is 'lonely', and its 'winding journey' is not merely into the light of day but 'through the day and time and *war* and history' (my italics). The little word 'war', slipped unobtrusively between 'time' and 'history' in the slow-moving final line punctuated by a repeated 'and', brings one with a shock of recognition up against the real reason for the despondency and futility in the poem – not only the poet's own sense of helplessness, but the present war in Europe and the re-enactment in it of the timeless conflicts of human history. At this point, we remember the serpent image of the engine's smoke and its echoing now in the winding stream. This journey into conflict is indeed a journey of betrayal into the loss of innocence and communal solidarity (*CP* 96).

'The River' continues the metaphor of the stream's historical journey. Here, the river's 'glass' is a mirror of human warring activity, showing the 'trained terrors' and 'well-practised partings' of a recurring pattern of violence and destruction. Hillsides are split open, the debris of human life 'strewn on the slope as by a wrecking wave / Among the grass and wild-flowers' (*CP* 97). Although vital and immediate, the imagery in this poem is not the kind of topical imagery associated with 'To J. F. H.'. Instead, we see Muir developing imagistic patterns which will become characteristic features of his mature style. There is the use of the conjunction 'and' to yoke seeming opposites and, in this yoking, to point to their inevitable relationship. In the river's mirror, 'harvest-home and Judgment Day of fire' are one, made synonymous by humankind's inability to desist from conflict. Another stylistic feature is the symbolic use of a negative image which derives its impact from the traditional everyday positive connotations within it. Thus the power of 'blackened field' and 'burning wood', like the unexpected conjunction of 'harvest-home' with 'Judgment Day of fire', is to a large extent due to the way in which the negative elements point to the contrary positive features implicit in the imagery: a field whose harvest should nourish and sustain; a wood whose trees should give shelter.

In the world of 'The River', these everyday sustaining values have been eroded. Ignorance and self-delusion dominate, and underlying these is a sense of humankind being driven onwards by some arbitrary fate to an ultimately futile goal:

> The disciplined soldiers come to conquer nothing,
> March upon emptiness and do not know
> Why all is dead and life has hidden itself.

The poem ends with the stream of history flowing onwards and the speaker asking 'what land', 'what space' it can possibly find 'far past the other side of the burning world' (*CP* 97).

In 'The Refugees', the hearthstone – traditionally an image of warmth, security and family solidarity – offers the first subversive note of the poem as the speaker looks backwards to find the seeds of the nightmare present in the indifference of the past. Like the family in the opening lines who 'lived in comfort in our haunted rooms' (*CP* 98), Muir and his wife. in the early 1920s, had lived self-containedly in the community of A. S. Neill's school at Hellerau, oblivious to the extent of the misery of many Germans as a consequence of the reparations demanded after the First World War and blind to the implications of the anti-Semitism which flourished unchecked in Germany and Austria.

Now, as with the story and photograph of the young Gestapo men whom he was later to encounter in Prague, events in Europe in the early 1940s seemed to provide a contemporary illustration of the biblical teaching about the sins of the fathers being visited upon the children.

This working-out of cause and effect is very much the context of 'The Refugees'. Like many of Muir's poems of this period, it is both topical and political, yet, as it develops, the investigation of good and evil and suffering in human life additionally takes on Calvinist connotations in its allusions to the Fall and Original Sin and in the symbolism of the 'red fruit hung ripe upon the bough':

> This is our punishment. We came
> Here without blame, yet with blame,
> Dark blame of others, but our blame also.
> This stroke was bound to fall,
> Though not to fall so . . .
>   Oh this is the taste
> Of evil done long since and always, quickened
> No one knows how
> While the red fruit hung ripe upon the bough
> And fell at last and rotted where it fell.
>
> (CP 96)

'The Refugees', as printed in *The Narrow Place*, is only one third of the original poem published in *New Alliance* in the autumn of 1939, a poem for which Muir had initially had high expectations but which in the end disappointed him. He wrote to Alec Aitken in January 1940 that 'it was inspired by quite sincere feeling but never rose to the right height, the pity and indignation never transmitted themselves, except in one or two lines in the last part'.[7] While this is certainly a just assessment of the principal part of the poem, his early optimism is, I think, justified by the reprinting of that 'last part', the Chorus of the original poem, which is ambivalent and haunting and points to the mystery of the human condition: our ignorance of our origins and of the way forward; the presence of suffering and of good and evil; our communal involvement in whatever life brings. Yet it is also a political poem of especial relevance to twentieth-century history and to a shrinking world where conflicts can no longer be isolated and contained but spill over to affect us all in our increasingly interdependent societies. The poem remains relevant beyond its wartime context into our late twentieth-century world, where, having been to a large extent

freed from the fear of imminent nuclear war, we find we are still plagued
by worldwide social and economic deprivation and by the 'dark blame of
others' and 'our blame also', as we face the legacy of the century's wars
in the outbreaks of regional schisms and internecine conflicts which
have come in the wake of the ending of the Cold War. We have yet to
'shape here a new philosophy' to deal with 'rejection bred by rejection /
Breeding rejection' (*CP* 99).

   The sense of constriction and unknown fate characteristic of the
earlier *Journeys and Places* is revived in this collection in poems such as
'The Human Fold', 'The Recurrence', 'The Wheel' and the eponymous
'The Narrow Place'. 'The Ring' and 'Scotland 1941' bring the theme of
disorder and disunity into the area of national life, and each opens with
a similar first line: 'Long since we were a family, a people'; 'We were a
tribe, a family, a people' (*CP* 112, 100). 'The Ring', written in a terza
rima form where the structural unity of the rhyming pattern ironically
counterpoints its theme of disunity, looks back to the neuroticism of
Muir's Glasgow days and forward to his *King Lear* essay and the
Labyrinth poem 'The Usurpers' in its animal metaphor of 'Lion and fox,
all dressed by fancy fine / In human flesh and armed with arrows and
spears'. As Muir was to argue in his essay in relation to the activities of
Goneril, Regan and Edmund, so in this poem he puts forward the view
that, when our ties of kinship and interdependence are broken, we
become human animals who live only in the present.

   Ties of kinship and a shared past are broken also in 'Scotland 1941'.
This poem belongs in theme with the pessimistic accounts of Scottish
life and history written by Muir in the 1930s and can probably be most
meaningfully discussed in Chapter 5 on 'Muir and Scotland'. Here, the
enemy is Calvinism, not the fascism of the Hitler period, but Muir finds
it to have been an equally destructive ideology leading to the loss of
nationhood and the growth of materialism and class conflict. In the
indigenous national context also, we need 'to shape a new philosophy'.
It is interesting to note in passing, however, that, as in his
confrontation with Europe at war, Muir's struggles with Scotland in
this poem provide a linguistically vital poetry – something applicable
also to the *One Foot in Eden* Scottish poems, 'The Incarnate One' and
'Scotland's Winter'.

   The Narrow Place also offers Muir's first reworking of the Penelope/
Odysseus legend to which he was to return again and again in his work.
As befits the predominantly anarchic context of the collection, the
emphasis in 'The Return of Odysseus' is on the disorder caused by the
absence of Odysseus:

> The doors flapped open in Odysseus' house,
> The lolling latches gave to every hand,
> Let traitor, babbler, tout and bargainer in.
>
> (*CP* 114)

The onomatopoeic quality in words and phrases such as 'flapped open', 'lolling latches', 'traitor, babbler, tout and bargainer' and 'spat' communicates the physical and social disintegration of Odysseus's home. The free, unrhymed verse-form patterns the lack of order in the events retold, while the image of the 'clean blue sea' frames this picture of present chaos with its connotations of a timeless, undefiled natural order. At the heart of this chaos sits Penelope 'at her chosen task, endless undoing / Of endless doing', a symbol of faith in an end unknown. Yet although Penelope is faithful, the main thrust of the poem is not towards this faithfulness but towards her lack of knowledge of the predestined way and her appeal for reassurance that her faithfulness will not prove to have been in vain:

> Oh will you ever return? Or are you dead,
> And this wrought emptiness my ultimate emptiness?
>
> (*CP* 115)

Powerful as Muir's enactment of human chaos is in this volume, it is not left to stand unopposed. In a time of severe international disorder about which the individual can do little and where there seems to be no foreseeable end to conflict, personal values and relationships may be our principal hold on the positives of human life. Muir has a keen sense of these positives, and they are to be found in the personal poems which bring *The Narrow Place* to a close. Outstanding among these personal poems is 'The Confirmation', a variation on the sonnet form with fifteen lines as opposed to fourteen and with the turn coming after the initial sestet as opposed to the traditional octave. Like its two companion poems, 'The Annunciation' and 'The Commemoration', it is a love-song to the poet's wife, and, as in Shakespeare's sonnet 'My mistress' eyes are nothing like the sun', it is not a conventional or unobtainable ideal which is celebrated here, but a worldly reality. The qualities which have proved their worth in a long marriage are defined in imagery which points to the essential attributes for life as we know it:

> But you,
> What shall I call you? A fountain in a waste,
> A well of water in a country dry,
> Or anything that's honest and good, an eye
> That makes the whole world bright. Your open heart,

Simple with giving, gives the primal deed,
The first good world, the blossom, the blowing seed,
The hearth, the steadfast land, the wandering sea,
Not beautiful or rare in every part,
But like yourself, as they were meant to be.

(CP 118)

The predominant note of *The Voyage*, which followed *The Narrow Place* in 1946, is philosophical and personal. There are fewer poems which would appear to have been directly inspired by the war situation, and the few war poems which are there are given a personal or philosophical orientation. In 'Reading in Wartime', for example, he turns to literature in the attempt to cope with the despair and futility engendered by war and finds his relief, characteristically, in the recognition of our common humanity which writers such as Samuel Johnson and Leo Tolstoy were able to communicate.

'Reading in Wartime' was one of three poems sent by Muir to Oscar Williams for inclusion in *The War Poets: An Anthology of the War Poetry of the Twentieth Century*. The others were 'The Escape' and 'The Lullaby', the latter being replaced eventually by the more striking poem 'The Rider Victory'. 'The Escape' is an interior a well as an actual journey, with the kind of imagery we have already seen in 'The River' where the traditional stability associated with its elements is evoked simultaneously with the depiction of its loss. Muir wrote to Williams that it had been suggested to him 'by a story called "Corporal Jack", an account of an English soldier's escape from prison camp, his wanderings through France, and his final arrival at Gibraltar' (*SL* 140). This reminded him of other wanderings throughout history such as those of the failed Crusades, and the story, as in many Muir scenarios, thus takes on a mythical identity. 'The Escape' additionally anticipates 'The Labyrinth' in its creation of a sense of entrapment, of roads which 'ran in a maze / Hither and thither, like a web', as the soldier tries to find a way over the line between 'the Occupied and Unoccupied'. Despite an initial semblance of normality in 'the family group / Still gathered round the dying hearth', this turns out to be an illusion. The hearth is 'dying'; the harvest-home is 'empty'. 'There was no promise in the bud, / No comfort in the blossoming tree':

In the church
In rows the stabled horses stood,
And the cottar's threshold stone
Was mired with earth and blood.

(CP 126–7)

Nor can there be moral certainty in a situation where right and wrong seem to have lost their clarity. The soldier asks himself: 'What is escape? and What is flight?' (*CP* 127).

Another war poem, 'The Rider Victory', is heraldic in imagery and would appear to have been inspired stylistically by Muir's reading of C. M. Bowra's *The Heritage of Symbolism*. He wrote to Stephen Spender in the summer of 1944 that Bowra's book had made him realise that he had been writing symbolist poetry himself for years without realising it. He added: 'He inspired me to write one deliberately, which I enclose' (*CP* 337). The opening, with its heroic portrait of rider and horse – 'The rider Victory reins his horse / Midway across the empty bridge' (*CP* 139) – could well stand as accompanying text for the great bronze and stone statues of conquering warriors of the past. Muir's poem, however, unlike its historical sculptural counterparts, belongs to a period in which consensus about such 'heroic' roles is not readily achieved. Thus we find that its subsequent imagery subverts rather than supports the majestic opening and shows the victory to be ultimately an empty one. The bridge and roads may be free, but horse and rider are 'halted in implacable air'; they have 'stony eyes'; the magnificent feat of sculpting the uprearing horse in the end is seen to have produced 'motionless statuary', the symbol, perhaps, of a futile victory. This sense of a victory which is meaningless in the context of spiritual values beyond immediate material objectives is assisted by the way in which from the beginning of the poem Muir creates a contrary spiritual subtext without explicitly defining it. Thus, even in the opening heroic portrait of uprearing horse and rider, we are told that the warrior has reined his horse 'as if head-tall he had met a wall'. The following insistence on the fact that 'there was nothing there at all, / No bodiless barrier, ghostly ridge' does not reassure but serves to reinforce the sense of the presence of unearthly values which would seem to have been left out of the reckoning, but which, inexplicably, as in Muir's later *Labyrinth* poem 'The Usurpers', make their troubling presence known. In the opening stanza, this presence is only hinted at, but in the next stanza it is deepened by the creation of an ironic context through language and imagery which have ambivalent connotations. 'The waiting kingdom' in mundane terms may be the country preparing to receive its new victorious ruler, but it also has connotations of another spiritual kingdom whose values have been forgotten here; the bridge and roads may seem to be free, but bridges are traditional symbols of actions irrevocably taken or of possible turning points. One already knows from Muir's poetry up to this point that for him roads are not free and straightforward, but twisting and deceiving and ultimately unknowable. The implicit irony in his initial depiction of heroic activity thus prepares us for the more overt message of the poem's ending with the 'motionless statuary' (*CP* 139) of rider and horse, an empty symbol so far as the search for true human significance is concerned and a potent reminder of the need for such a search in time of war.

'The Return of the Greeks' also points to the way in which war and the attitudes engendered by war distort and destroy essential human values. In this version of the Penelope and Odysseus legend, the emphasis is not on the two principal characters but on the ordinary fighting men who went to the siege of Troy and have now come home 'sleepwandering from the war' (*CP* 125). Their experience during these war years has been so narrowed, and yet so intensified, that they are now alienated from normal life, which seems diminished, both physically and philosophically. Everything seems 'trite and strange'; 'a childish scene'. Most seriously from the point of view of Muir's belief in the essential relationship between past and present and the importance of maintaining such continuity, the Greeks can no longer accept what now seems to them to be a meaningless connection:

> The past and the present bound
> In one oblivious round
> Past thinking trite and strange.
>   (*CP* 126)

The poem's basic metre is iambic trimeter with a change to a trochee or spondee pattern when emphasis is wanted on specific words such as 'weakened' or 'blundering' or on the double stress of 'ten years'. While one might expect such a short metrical line to be fast-moving, the verses are given a heavy rhythmic movement by the use of polysyllabic words and clogging consonants, such as 'sleepwandering' and 'blundering', which communicate the weariness and reluctance of the returning Greeks. The intensity and obsessive nature of their experience is conveyed in phrases such as 'nothing there at all / But an alley steep and small, / Tramped earth and towering stone'. The rhyme pattern adds to the sense of entrapment with its circular *ababba* movement, the last word in the final line of each verse repeating the last word of the first line. The poem ends with Penelope still 'alone in her tower' awaiting the return of Odysseus, but with the suggestion that the Greek veterans themselves are hesitantly reaccepting their place in the circle of past and present, a suggestion implicitly communicated through Muir's coupling of the contradictory elements in their responses:

Penelope in her tower
Looked down upon the show
And saw within an hour
Each man to his wife go,
Hesitant, sure and slow: [my italics]
She, alone in her tower.

(*CP* 126)

Another poem which explores the effect of a timeless experience
outside the bounds of what we call normal life is the eponymous 'The
Voyage'. This poem had its source in a story told to Muir by the novelist
Eric Linklater, of a sea voyage to Australia which, because of bad
weather, was unrelieved by the sighting of any other ship and which
lasted so long that the sailors began to speculate that perhaps the world
had come to an end and that they alone were left alive.[8] Inevitably, the
poem evokes the world of Coleridge's 'The Ancient Mariner', an
association assisted by its ballad-like verse-form. As in Coleridge's
poem, the isolation and the accompanying mesmerised speculation of
the sailors produce their own visions. In 'The Voyage', however, the
vision is not of a death-ship, given shape by the Mariner's guilt-ridden
conscience, but an idealised vision of the sights and sounds of home:
'the whispering quays' of a safe harbour; 'a land of harvests and of graves'
(*CP* 135) – the latter image both capturing the cycle of life in a
philosophical sense and imaging in a concrete visual way the Orkney
landscape with its ancient, domed burial chambers patterned in the
similarly domed haystacks of late summer.

As their visions suggest, Muir's sailors are not Coleridge's. Their
isolation – brought about not by evil action but mysteriously given to
them – becomes a peace and a blessing; the homeland of their visions
becomes a 'lengendary land' and their present 'loss . . . our only joy'
(*CP* 136). Yet, as with T. S. Eliot's moment in the rose garden in
'Burnt Norton' and his insight that 'humankind / Cannot bear very
much reality'[9] – what MacDiarmid also characterised memorably in *A
Drunk Man Looks at the Thistle* as 'men canna look on nakit licht'[10] – so
Muir's enactment of a visionary reality beyond human time cannot last.
Landfall is eventually made, and the sailors return, with some sense of
loss, to the flawed world of everyday human experience. The sailors are
thus in one sense patterning the experience of the sleepwandering
Greeks. Yet, although the effect of the experiences would seem initially
and superficially to be similar, in that both groups of travellers make
landfall reluctantly and with some sense of loss, each experience is
essentially different, as are the reasons for the disappointment. The

sailors have experienced the 'clear unfallen world' and 'radiant kingdom' of Muir's later poem 'The Transfiguration', and there is inevitably a sense of loss as 'the world / Rolled back into its place, and we are here' (*CP* 185–6). In 'The Return of the Greeks', on the other hand, the intense experience of war has distorted human values and broken the communal bonds on which human life is built and which sustain it. The sense of loss in the Greek poem is for the loss of an intense but ultimately destructive experience, and the apparently trite shadow-world of home life is in fact the necessary, even if flawed, human context to which we all belong. Taken together, these poems point to two consistent features of Muir's work: the search for the fable behind the human story and the simultaneous insistence on the significance of the world of that human story. Muir's vision is at one and the same time transcendental and of this world.

As in *The Narrow Place*, *The Voyage* contains a number of personal poems which give expression to what can be achieved 'in Time's despite' (*CP* 150). The faith in the power of human love which is given expression in these poems is restated in Muir's letter to Stephen Spender of 21 March 1944:

> For me too love is the supreme quality and more closely connected with immortality than any other, immortality either as you or I conceive it. And in a way I feel it is more important than immortality. If I could really love all creatures and all things I should not trouble about immortality. (*SL* 138)

'In Love for Long' and 'A Birthday' are two of the poems which give expression to this feeling of love for 'all creatures and all things'. Willa Muir tells that both poems were written on the Pentland Hills near Swanston, and, in a BBC 'Chapbook' programme in 1952, Muir himself described how 'In Love for Long' came out of an experience at Swanston when he felt 'an unmistakable warm feeling for the ground I was sitting on, as if I were in love with the earth itself, and the clouds, and the soft subdued light'.[11] 'A Birthday' evokes more specifically and sensuously the world of nature, an infrequent attribute of Muir's poetry, but welcome when it comes, as here, in

> The tingling smell and touch
> Of dogrose and sweet briar,
> Nettles against the wall,
> All sours and sweets that grow
> Together or apart
> In hedge or marsh or ditch.

The second stanza returns to the rightness of childhood's vision as imaged in the Wyre section of his autobiography and in poems such as 'Childhood' and 'The Myth':

> The first look and the last
> When all between has passed
> Restore ingenuous good

and to a positive expression of his recurring theme that man's true journey through life has been mapped out for him and he made for it:

> Before I touched the food
> Sweetness ensnared my tongue;
> Before I saw the wood
> I loved each nook and bend,
> The track going right and wrong;
> Before I took the road
> Direction ravished my soul.
>
> (*CP* 152)

The volume ends with 'In Love for Long' and its Blakean metaphor of what can be held 'in Time's despite':

> This love a moment known
> For what I do not know
> And in a moment gone
> Is like the happy doe
> That keeps its perfect laws
> Between the tiger's paws
> And vindicates its cause.
>
> (*CP* 154)

This is a vision which Muir found it almost impossible to maintain when he entered the labyrinth of postwar Europe in 1945.

II

The Labyrinth

At the end of the war, Muir was appointed Director of the British Institute in Prague by the British Council, and in August 1945 he set out for the city which had been associated with his new freedom in the 1920s. He found a Europe ravaged by war and a Prague which was 'the same and yet not the same, whose streets I or someone very like me had walked many years before' (*A* 255). This ambivalent response to the city

anticipated the 'lost way' theme of many of the poems written during
his period in Czechoslovakia, while his journey through Germany to
Prague provided the actuality of the experiences imagined in poems
such as 'The Refugees' and 'The River' from the earlier *Narrow Place*
collection:

> When we reached Germany there seemed to be nothing unmarked
> by the war: the towns in ruins, the roads and fields scarred and
> deserted. It was like a country where the population had become
> homeless, and when we met occasional family groups on the roads
> they seemed to be on a pilgrimage from nowhere to nowhere. In
> the towns and far out in the countryside we met them pushing
> their belongings on hand-carts, with a look of dull surprise on
> their faces. Few trains were running; the great machine was
> broken; and the men, but for the women and children following
> them, might have been survivors of one of the mediaeval crusades
> wandering back across Europe to seek their homes. Now by all
> appearances there were no homes for them to seek. (*A* 251)

Although the Muirs were aware of undercurrents in the Prague
atmosphere — what Willa Muir called 'the opaqueness, the alien
inscrutability we felt in the atmosphere of Prague, despite our
friendliness and personal popularity' — they did not understand their
source. Willa acknowledged that

> the basic assumption of believing that the political line of division
> ran between Germany, the enemy, on one side and all the Allies,
> including Russia, on the other, was one that Edwin and I made
> unthinkingly. It never occurred to us at the time that Stalin might
> already be deepening a cleavage, as with a sword, between
> America, together with her European Allies, and Russia. (*B* 218)

This postwar European experience is the context of *The Labyrinth*, a
volume distinguished by the immediacy and intensity of its poetic
communication and the maturity of its technique. It may be that Muir's
teaching at Charles University made him more conscious of formal
considerations in relation to his own work. He wrote to William
Montgomerie in March 1946:

> I have been lecturing twice a week to the English class at the
> Charles University (I call it a class, but it is more like a
> demonstration, comprising several hundred students, without
> books, so that I have to *create* Wordsworth, Coleridge, Blake, and
> the others for them . . . I have to explain the poems to them, of
> course, build up Blake's Tiger, find some definite meaning in the
> 'deeps' and 'skies', and I find this very interesting, useful for the
> students, and very good for myself as a critic, since it forces me to

keep my eye perpetually on the object, and almost on every word.
(*SL* 140)

Letters from this period refer to his attempt 'to write poetry that was both simple and unexpected', to an intention to call a new collection 'Symbols, or something of that kind, for they all deal with symbolical human situations and types' (*SL* 146). Whatever the reason, *The Labyrinth* demands and repays the kind of stylistic analysis which one accepts as normal practice in relation to a modernist such as Eliot, but which is less often given to Muir's work.

'The Labyrinth' is the principal statement of the 'lost way' theme in the volume. It opens with a sentence thirty-five lines in length, in which the thread of meaning is continually being obscured by complex syntax and parenthetical comments. That this was deliberate methodology is shown by Muir's own comments on the poem which had been begun at the Writers' House at Dobris in Czechoslovakia:

> Thinking there of the old story of the labyrinth of Cnossos and the journey of Theseus through it and out of it, I felt that this was an image of human life with its errors and ignorance and endless intricacy. In the poem I made the labyrinth stand for all this. . . . The poem begins with a very long sentence, deliberately labyrinthine, to give the mood'.[12]

'The Labyrinth' is therefore not a retelling of the Theseus myth but rather a psychological drama inspired by it.

The referential context of the poem is unusually rich and allusive. Dostoyevsky's novel *The Double*, with its intuition of the 'double' in the human psyche, is evoked by the Golyadkin-like experience of the 'swift recoils, so many I almost feared / I'd meet myself returning at some smooth corner, / Myself or my ghost' (*CP* 157), as is the premonition of death traditionally associated with a meeting with one's doppelgänger or other self. At times, the maze alters its centre of gravity and, like the old wheel of fate, 'revolved around me on its hidden axis'. K's frustrated efforts to reach the Castle and its ruler in Kafka's *The Castle* are called to mind in the description of

> all the roads
> That run through the noisy world, deceiving streets
> That meet and part and meet, and rooms that open
> Into each other — and never a final room —
> Stairways and corridors and antechambers
> That vacantly wait for some great audience.
> (*CP* 158)

In yet another version of the labyrinth motif, 'the smooth sea-tracks that open and close again' (*CP* 158) take us into the world of the *Narrow Place* poem 'The Swimmer's Death' and the loneliness of human suffering.

After the halting, syntactically blocked movement of the long opening depiction of the labyrinth, the verse movement quickens as the protagonist wildly attempts, as in a nightmare, to escape the maze:

> And then I'd stumble
> In sudden blindness, hasten, almost run,
> As if the maze itself were after me
> And soon must catch me up.
>
> (*CP* 158)

However, he can no more escape the maze than could the speaker of the early 'Original Place' 'leave these fields' (*CP* 90). Muir adds to the sense of claustrophobic hopelessness at this point through the specious counsel of the 'bad spirit' who, like Despaire in Spenser's *The Faerie Queene*, attempts to remove any remaining show of resistance:

> 'No, do not hurry.
> No need to hurry. Haste and delay are equal
> In this one world, for there's no exit, none,
> No place to come to, and you'll end where you are,
> Deep in the centre of the endless maze.'
>
> (*CP* 158)

In its opening section, 'The Labyrinth' thus gives form to the sense of insecurity and hopelessness experienced by Muir in postwar Prague, to his awareness of new beginnings thwarted and human potential and openness crushed. It is not, of course, necessary to tie the poem to Prague in its interpretation. For Peter Butter, for example, it 'deals with Muir's state of alienation in his Glasgow years, his escape from it and his later efforts to reconcile apparently contradictory conceptions of human life'.[13] Nor does our response to the poem depend on autobiographical interpretation or the recognition of associations such as those mentioned above. The images of restriction and human vulnerability validate themselves. As we have seen, the 'lost way' theme is a recurring preoccupation in Muir's work. What the Prague experience did was give it new definition and immediacy, bringing Muir's personal life story into conjunction with the sufferings of postwar Europe.

'The Labyrinth' has attracted much critical attention, especially in relation to its picture of the gods. As in Hölderlin's 'Hyperions

Schiksaalslied', Muir's gods walk above in the light ('Ihr wandelt droben im Licht') while, as we have seen in the labyrinth passages of the poem, suffering mortals fall

> Blindlings von einer
> > Stunde zur andern,
> > > Wie Wasser von Klippe
> > > > Zu Klippe geworfen,
> > > > > Jahr lang ins Ungewisse hinab.[14]

(Blindly from one hour to the next,
Flung like water from crag to crag
Downwards for years into uncertainty.)

Muir himself said of the labyrinth/gods antithesis in his poem: 'But I wanted also to give an image of the life of the gods, to whom all that is confusion down here is clear and harmonious as seen eternally'.[15]

In their readings of 'The Labyrinth' poem, Peter Butter and Christopher Wiseman both accept the validity of the portrayal of the gods. For Butter, 'this is the real world, one in which time is contained within eternity rather than being opposed to it',[16] while Wiseman finds a 'redemptive authenticity' in the vision of the gods. For him, this vision is 'an expansion of the lines in the early poem "The Mythical Journey" . . . The gods preside over a place of harmony . . . and the labyrinth, in comparison, becomes small and inconsequential'.[17]

On the other hand, it could be argued that such readings are conditioned by an acceptance of Muir's Christianity (and perhaps by the critic's own religious viewpoint) and that they underestimate the stylistic evidence of the poem. For it is the communication of the labyrinth nightmare which in poetic terms tells most about human experience. The labyrinth poetry is strong, richly allusive, varied in movement, pulsing with life. In contrast, the vision of the gods appears lifeless, a wistful substitution of wish-fulfilment for actuality. There is a lack of poetic intensity which stems, I believe, from the imposed nature of the reconciliation vision. Elizabeth Huberman, whose reading of Muir's work most often envisages a progression from darkness to the light of *One Foot in Eden*, is nevertheless also dissatisfied with 'The Labyrinth' gods, finding that 'Muir's view of the reconciling gods derives from outside'.[18] In addition, one could argue that this vision of the gods is philosophically more terrifying than the experience of life's labyrinth which he so potently evokes. There is something irreconcilably fearful in the idea of the gods so serenely overlooking the toy-sized activities of our human world. One remembers Hugh MacDiarmid's contrary vision in 'The Snares of Varuna' section of *In Memoriam James*

Joyce, which also derives from the nightmare experience of Europe in the twentieth century:

> The world is fast bound in the snares of Varuna
> – 'Cords consisting of serpents' . . .
> . . . The winkings of men's eyes
> Are all numbered by him; he wields the universe
> As gamesters handle dice.[19]

This itself contains an echo of Gloucester's cry: 'As flies to wanton boys, are we to the gods; / They kill us for their sport' (IV i 36–7). Muir's essential response to the problems of evil and human mortality is, I believe, more fairly and satisfyingly represented by his letter to Stephen Spender from Edinburgh in March 1944. He writes to Spender:

> The problems are terrifying, as you say. The religions exist, I suppose, to provide an explanation of them. I can't accept any religious explanation that I know of, any more than you. I would rather have the problems themselves, for from an awareness of them and their vastness I get some sort of living experience, some sense even of communion, of being in the whole in some way, whereas from the explanations I should only get comfort and reassurance and a sense of safety which I know is not genuine.
> (*SL* 137)

This comment seems especially relevant to an evaluation of his aims and achievement in 'The Labyrinth'.

The poem ends, as it began, with the intensity of the labyrinth experience reasserting itself poetically over the previous vision of reconciliation. After the quiescence of the 'real world' of the gods, the speaker returns to

> the lie,
> The maze, the wild-wood waste of falsehood, roads
> That run and run and never reach an end,
> Embowered in error.
>
> (*CP* 159)

The linguistic and rhythmic vigour of the writing here makes its own artistic point, while the final message of the poem is ambivalent in its mingling of dream and reality:

> Last night I dreamt I was in the labyrinth,
> And woke far on. I did not know the place
> (*CP* 159)

In addition to the opposing labyrinth and gods symbolism, there is also within the world of human experience in the poem the possibility of a compensatory vision. As in Neil M. Gunn's late novels of disintegration in the modern world, nature in Muir's poem provides a restorative counterbalance:

> ever since I came out
> To the world, the still fields swift with flowers, the trees
> All bright with blossom, the little green hills, the sea,
> The sky and all in movement under it,
> Shepherds and flocks and birds and the young and old . . .
>
> (*CP* 157)

This moment of refreshment is not dependent on supernatural factors, and its success in poetic terms speaks for its validity. It, like the terror of the labyrinth, is part of the world of living experience, an insight which Muir develops more fully in the *One Foot in Eden* collection.

'The Way', 'The Return' and 'The Journey Back' continue the 'lost way' theme while simultaneously searching for a positive outcome. The leitmotiv of the antiphonal 'The Way' is that there is no way back: 'The Way leads on' (*CP* 159). 'The Return' is based on one of the dreams which came with Muir's psychoanalysis in the early 1920s and is a more mature version of another of his recurring themes: that of tracing backwards in memory and imagination the events of his life in the effort to come to terms with them. Here, the metaphor is a domestic one as the poet returns as an old man 'to the house / Of my own life' (*CP* 160). Memory is the meeting-place where his past and present, 'childhood and youth and manhood', can welcome each other: 'There all the doors stand open / Perpetually, and the rooms ring with sweet voices . . . and not a room but is / My own, beloved and longed for'. Yet, when he finally reaches the house, he finds he 'cannot enter, for all within / Rises before me there, rises against me'. However much one might want to re-enter the past, to relive one's life in a more positive way, there is no going back. 'That journey's done' (*CP* 160, 159).

'The Journey Back' has aroused many laudatory critical responses. Kathleen Raine considers it 'Muir's greatest poem',[20] and she is supported by Elizabeth Jennings ('Muir's finest poem')[21] and Peter Butter ('one of his greatest' poems).[22] For James Aitchison, it is 'the prophetic vision of a mature artist at the height of his powers'.[23] Elizabeth Huberman, on the other hand, finds a failure to 'trust the basic metaphor'[24] in this poem, as in 'The Labyrinth', and contrasts this unfavourably with the third poem in Rainer Maria Rilke's *Duino Elegies*, to which Muir's opening would appear to refer. Christopher Wiseman's reading, which interprets the journey as 'a journey in more than one direction',[25] seems to point to ambiguity in the imagery.

In its formal organisation into seven contrasting movements, the poem is reminiscent of the early *Variations on a Time Theme* and of T. S. Eliot's method in *The Waste Land* and *Four Quartets* of overcoming the structural problems posed by the long poem. Its length suggests that Muir was consciously attempting an ambitious work, as does the echo of Rilke in its opening lines. Yet the poem as a whole does not seem to me to sustain the promise of its opening metaphor of 'old founts dried up whose rivers run far on / Through you and me' (*CP* 161) – a metaphor which leads one to expect the kind of imaginative exploration of sources to be found in Neil M. Gunn's fine novel *Highland River*, Hugh MacDiarmid's 'Muckle Toon' poetry of the 1930s, or, indeed, in Rilke himself. There is a lack of coherence both within individual movements and in the pattern of the whole. The first poem, for example, divides into two contrasting sections. In its fine opening, Muir states the 'old founts' metaphor then follows this through in a journey back not only to the house of his own life, as in 'The Return', but also into the lives of his father and forefathers. He envisages these forefathers as dried-up rivers whose waters now run through him, just as the yet unknown future will in its turn become fertilised by the waters of present lives as they fall back to become the past.

The speaker sets out, then, to explore that first of Muir's 'mysteries', the 'where we came from' of *An Autobiography*. Once past his father's 'friendly station', however, things begin to wrong for the searcher and stylistically for his poet: 'all is strange', and the poet/traveller is once again in the labyrinth nightmare, 'locked inside / The savage keep, the grim rectangular tower / From which the fanatic neighbour-hater scowls'. He finds himself falling 'to gasp and choke in the cramped miser's body'. He imagines a murderer ancestor and is obsessed by

> those hands
> That shall be always with me, serve my ends,
> Button, unbutton for my body's needs,
> Are intimate with me, the officious tools
> That wash my face, push food into my mouth
> Loathed servants fed from my averted heart.
>   (*CP* 162)

Why should there be such a melodramatic selection of negative characters to represent the ancestors he finds on his journey back, one has to ask? Why the intensity of disgust at bodily needs and functions? There seems to be an almost pathological obsession here, the source of which is unclear and appears to lie outwith the poem.

Rilke's 'Elegy' also has its violent ancestral moments:

> Verliess es, ging die
> eigenen Wurzeln hinaus in gewaltigen Ursprung,
> wo seine kleine Geburt schon überlebt war.[26]

> (Left it, continued
> out through his own roots into violent beginning
> where his tiny birth was already outlived.)

In Rilke, however, these are contained within the overall metaphor of love – of sexual love between man and woman and protective mother-love between mother and male child. His metaphor is coherently developed, and individual images do not appear to be arbitrary and contrived or to stem from some unresolved personal conflict as in Muir's poem.

In the poem sequence as a whole, there are too many unrelated images and influences to make for a satisfactory, resolved communication. The second poem is more of a unity with a fine, hypnotic, rhythmic movement and mythic context, moving away from the negative specificity of the first poem into a spirit presence. Yet, although the rhythmic movement is songlike and haunting, the imagery lacks freshness and again seems contrived: 'countless wanderings'; 'silver scars / Of blanched and dying stars'; 'well-bred animal / With coat of seemly mail'. It may be, as has been suggested, that the 'consternations' of the second stanza intends a pun on the German word for star, Stern – but, if so, this seems an obvious, somewhat banal device (*CP* 163).

The third poem returns to the motif of journeying backwards, this time into a pre-Christian and even prehistory period. There is again something fanciful in the idea of the speaker watching himself lay his dead self in the grave and carry out the funeral rituals, while the last line of this poem 'The red rose blooms and moulders by the wall' leads one into the fin-de-siècle imagery of the fourth poem with its 'through the air descends a dust / Blown from the scentless desert of dead time'; 'I toss / Remembrance and rememberer all confused / In a light fume' (*CP* 165). This has the air of escapist romance found in Rossetti as opposed to being a logical follow-through of the philosophical journey begun in the first poem. The original starting point seems lost sight of in the fifth poem also, where, with echoes of Eliot, a Tiresias-like speaker observes and comments on 'the calamities of an age' (*CP* 165) which has many resemblances to the contemporary war-torn context. Hölderlin's gods reappear in the sixth terza rima movement, once again walking 'high in their mountainland in light'. This would appear to represent a parallel moment of insight and tranquility to the vision of the gods in 'The Labyrinth', but it does not facilitate the logical process of the original journey, and again the imagery seems limp and conventional: 'tranquil round'; 'tongues in silence overflow'; 'following a falling star' (*CP* 166). One has only to contrast this with a passage such as Eliot's moment in the rose garden in 'Burnt Norton' or the hypnotic, symbolic 'Garlic and sapphires in the mud' movement from the same poem to perceive the absence of vital poetic imagination in Muir's sequence. Eliot's *Four Quartets*, with their spiritual, philosophical quest, may well have been in Muir's mind as he put together his own poem, and it is the speculative tone of Eliot's voice which opens the seventh poem. In this poem, an attempt is made to draw the sequence back into the pattern of its opening metaphor with the familiar theme of the lost way and how it is to be found. The most convincing insight of the seven movements is to be found here with its 'how could I come / To where I am but by that deafening road . . . by which all come to all . . .?' (*CP* 166). Its 'golden harvester' conclusion, however, retreats once more into hazy poetic statement and does not appear to evolve out of any logical process within the poem sequence as a whole.

I have spent time on this poem because of the high claims which have been made for it and the accompanying absence of extended substantiation of these claims. Christopher Wiseman and Roger Knight are two critics who have attempted substantiation. Wiseman, who is on most occasions a perceptive critic, tries too hard and finds himself lost in a biographical journey which seems to be travelling in several directions simultaneously and which takes in Glasgow, 'the ghastly bone factory in Greenock', Eden, the Fall and the 1939–45 war. This makes a nonsense of the opening metaphor, and the comment on individual sections does not appear to justify the claim that the sequence contains 'some of his greatest writing'.[27] Knight makes similar claims, but avoids biographical analysis, turning instead to spiritual texts such as the Upanishads for substantiation. This puts emphasis on the transcendental but seems to me to be no more convincing in relation to an assessment of the imaginative quality of the imagery and poetic insight. Elizabeth Huberman seems the only critic with the courage to proclaim that this emperor has no clothes, and the substantiation of her view that the sequence lacks 'unity of development'[28] is undertaken with clarity of illustration and argument.

Muir can be a fine poet, and there are many fine poems in *The Labyrinth* collection, but I believe that there is too often a tendency in criticism of his work to accept that a high, spiritual, symbolically-defined theme must result in a major, significant poem (Arnold, with

his insistence on the 'sublime' subject, believed likewise). This can do
his reputation no service. He is in my view much more successful when
he eschews the long poem-sequence format found here and in the earlier
Variations on a Time Theme, where individual poems have not been
composed at the same time or originally conceived as a linked sequence.
'The Journey Back' fits more readily into the earlier pattern of mythical
journeys than it does into the more coherently-developed themes of *The
Labyrinth*.

Several poems in the collection derive more directly from Muir's
experiences in postwar Prague. Among these are 'The Interrogation',
'The Good Town', 'The Usurpers', 'The Helmet' and 'The Combat'.

In *An Autobiography*, Muir describes both the increasing tension
in Prague as the communists began to tighten their grip on
Czechoslovakia, and the parliamentary crisis of early 1948 which
preceded the final putsch. In the days immediately before the takeover,
the situation was like that satirised by Karl Kraus in *Die Fackel* in the
years before Hitler came to power in Germany:

> The stories kept coming in: a high Russian official had arrived in
> Prague just before the trouble began: Beneš had been prevented
> from speaking to the people over the radio. When people do not
> believe what is said by the newspapers, they create their news for
> themselves. (A 266)

As Karl Kraus had acknowledged the defeat of satire when Hitler came
to power in 1933 – 'Mir fällt zu Hitler nichts ein'; 'Ich bleibe stumm' ('I
can do nothing with Hitler'; 'I remain silent')[29] – so too was postwar
Prague emasculated in the face of the communist putsch:

> The old stale fears were back. No one opened his mouth in the
> trams. No one said 'God damn the government,' knowing he
> would be arrested if he did. No one dared to tell what he really
> thought, except in his own house or to a friend he could trust. No
> one telephoned if he could help it, though in a very short time
> people knew by the slight diminution in the volume of sound
> when the line was being tapped. And men at last became
> suspicious even of their friends. (A 267)

This is the context which gave rise to poems such as 'The Good
Town' and 'The Interrogation'. The former has been criticised by the
poet Edwin Morgan for its simplistic opposition of good and evil and
what he calls its 'Danny Kaye "streets of friendly neighbours" where
lock and key were "quaint antiquities fit for museums" while ivy trailed
"across the prison door"'.[30] There is certainly justification for such
criticism in the poem's opening section. However, as it proceeds, this
initial disability is overcome, so that the ultimate, overriding

communication is what Muir himself described as 'something that was happening in Europe'.[31] As in 'The Refugees' from *The Narrow Place*, 'The Good Town' forces the reader to reconsider the values of his or her society and ask the question: 'how did it happen?'

> How did it come?
> From outside, so it seemed, an endless source,
> Disorder inexhaustible, strange to us,
> Incomprehensible. Yet sometimes now
> We ask ourselves, we the old citizens:
> 'Could it have come from us? Was our peace peace?
> Our goodness goodness?'
>
> (*CP* 175)

'The Interrogation' is even more topically presented: a couple or a group of people are caught by a chance meeting with a police or government patrol and are subjected to interrogation:

> We could have crossed the road but hesitated,
> And then came the patrol;
> The leader conscientious and intent,
> The men surly, indifferent.
> While we stood by and waited
> The interrogation began . . .
>
> (*CP* 172)

The atmosphere of tension and unbearable waiting communicated here is to a large extent achieved through rhythmic movement, in the long, slow final line, for example: 'And still the interrogation is going on', and throughout the poem in silent beats or pauses at the end or in the middle of lines which insist on being taken into account. This sense of waiting is assisted by the irregular rhyming pattern where words 'chime' only infrequently, as in 'hesitated' with the long gap before 'waited'. In contrast are the quick, agitated rhythms of the questioning – 'who, what we are, / Where we have come from, with what purpose . . .'. Another factor in the poem is the *chance* nature of the happenings: 'We *could* have crossed the road but *hesitated*, / And then came the patrol'. The very ordinariness of this happening seems to increase our involvement with the events, as does the fact that the arrest and questioning is taking place while other people go about their everyday business. Nature, too, is indifferent to the human drama – 'The thoughtless field is near' – and, as in Muir's early poems of restricted, predestined fate, so here the protagonists 'cannot choose / Answer or action' (*CP* 172–3). Postwar Prague showed him that arbitrary, impersonal vengeance was not the prerogative of a Calvinist God.

'The Usurpers' continues the theme of the destruction of traditional values and freedoms by the imposition of an impersonal, authoritarian regime. The poem is closely related to Muir's W. P. Ker Memorial Lecture, 'The Politics of *King Lear*', delivered at the University of Glasgow in 1946 and reprinted in *Essays on Literature and Society*. In this essay, Muir saw the evil perpetrated by Lear's daughters and their associates as coming from a society in a 'violent period of transition' when 'the modern individualist world was bringing itself to birth'. As opposed to a Shakespearean character such as Macbeth who belongs to the old order of society and so can still feel guilt for his political crimes, the sisters in *King Lear* 'never feel that they have done wrong, and this is because they represent a new idea; and new ideas, like everything new, bring with them their own kind of innocence' (*ELS* 35). To Lear, however, his daughters are 'unnatural', and it is this 'unnatural' theme which dominates both the ending of the essay and the later 'Usurpers' poem.

In Muir's view, Goneril, Regan and Edmund are 'divested of all associations, denuded of memory' (*ELS* 43). They have become human animals, living in 'this shallow present' where 'words are their teeth and claws, and action the technique of the deadly spring' (*ELS* 43, 45). The Usurpers are similarly 'self-guided, self-impelled and self-sustained': 'Our thoughts are deeds; we dare do all we think, / Since there's no one to check us, here or elsewhere' (*CP* 176). They too have pushed aside the old loyalties and inherited traditions in favour of a political system where 'categories', not people, signify, and where self-interest is the guiding principle. Yet, as Muir's scenario develops, we find that these new men protest too much, that they are not entirely at ease with their 'freedom'. They cannot quite dispel the 'old garrulous ghosts' of the world of dreams, that world of the unconscious to which Muir always looked for self-knowledge. Nature, too, unsettles them, as we see in the following passage, where the insistent repetition of 'us', 'upon us', 'judge us', 'against us' proclaims both the self-absorption of the new men and their simultaneous, almost Wordsworthian awareness of Nature's 'severer interventions':[32]

> The day itself sometimes works spells upon us
> And then the trees look unfamiliar. Yet
> It is a lie that they are witnesses,
> That the mountains judge us, brooks tell tales upon us.
> We have thought sometimes the rocks looked strangely on us

Have fancied that the waves were angry with us,
Heard dark runes murmuring in the autumn wind,
Muttering and murmuring like old toothless women
That prophesied against us in ancient tongues.

(*CP* 177)

In terms of Muir's philosophy, such a regime cannot produce a healthy
society but can lead only to 'abstract calamity' for human beings. He
used this phrase in the poem 'The Incarnate One' from the *One Foot in
Eden* collection in relation to the impersonality of a Calvinist religion
which destroyed the humanity of Christ and of human life, but it is
equally applicable to his observation of totalitarian systems – both
communist and fascist – in mid-twentieth-century Europe. As early as
1934, Muir had published an article in the *European Quarterly* entitled
'Bolshevism and Calvinism', in which he pointed to the 'decisive
resemblance between Calvinism and Bolshevism' which lay

> in their working logic . . . its acceptance of determinism as a
> working hypothesis and, secondly, its exclusiveness. It is the logic
> of a class (in the first case the elect, in the second the proletariat)
> and so possesses an enormous functional efficiency; but it is also the
> logic of a class convinced that its eventual success is certain and
> unavoidable.

He saw both as cutting themselves off from European civilisation and
both 'preferred the claims of the mass to those of the individual,
exercising a strict control over people's private affairs'.[33]

In the communism which Muir experienced in Prague, therefore,
what alienated him most was this disregard for the worth of the
individual. In *An Autobiography*, for example, he describes the 'choice'
presented by the communist authorities to a Czech woman whose
husband had been killed in the Resistance. She could either join the
Party or lose her job and pension which supported not only herself but
also her invalid parents. For the new rulers, the way forward may have
seemed clear, but it took no account of individual human circumstances: 'Her parents, who like herself were Catholics, would not speak
to her again if she became a Communist; if she did not, they would
starve. The problem was completely impersonal, and completely
insoluble' (*A* 268).

For Muir,

> impersonality is an admirable quality in a historian, so long as he
> has human understanding as well. But to observe the long struggle
> of humanity as one observes a scientific demonstration heats the
> brains of men and petrifies their hearts; and to deal impersonally

with the living human beings around us or beneath us, knowing that we have the power to do so, is merely a particular form of inhumanity. (*A* 269)

Such were the happenings and stories of past happenings which the Muirs encountered during this second sojourn in Prague. They gave rise to poems such as 'The Helmet' and 'The Combat', which continue his exploration of evil in human society and the courage with which the human spirit can resist it. Both poems have a simple, ballad-like form which belies the complexity of their content. Willa Muir said of 'The Combat' that it had been inspired by a Czech friend (perhaps the woman in Muir's own account?) who, although 'threatened with the loss of her small widow's pension if she did not join the Party, said one must never lose faith, never give up hope' (*B* 238). Muir himself describes their attendance at a church service in the outskirts of the little town of Piĕstany and his observation of an old peasant woman kneeling in front of them: 'my eyes came back again and again to the worn and patched soles of her boots, a battered image of her own constancy and humble faith. I did not feel that this ancient humanity could ever be destroyed by the new order' (*A* 272).

This would seem to be the message of 'The Combat' also. Opposed in a recurring combat in which neither side is indubitably the victor are 'a crested animal in his pride', a medieval mythical beast with 'body of leopard, eagle's head / And whetted beak, and lion's mane . . .' and

A soft round beast as brown as clay;
All rent and patched his wretched skin;
A battered bag he might have been,
Some old used thing to throw away.

(*CP* 170)

The poem is one which is based on the dream visions which occurred during Muir's analysis in the 1920s, and the symbolic fight described would appear to be the eternally recurring battle between good and evil. As with Muir's observation of the old peasant woman in Piĕstany, the poem leaves one with a sense of the indestructibility of the human spirit, despite repeated assaults upon it. Its message anticipates also the faith of the Czech playwright Václav Havel, much imprisoned under the communists and until recently president of the communist-free Czechoslovakia. In his 'Letter to Dr Gustáv Husák', written in 1975, Havel, like Muir, points to the unquenchable vitality within the human spirit. He says:

life may be subjected to a prolonged and thorough process of violation, enfeeblement and anaesthesia. Yet, in the end, it cannot be permanently halted. Albeit quietly, covertly and slowly, it nevertheless goes on. Though it be estranged from itself a thousand times, it always manages in some way to recuperate; however violently ravished, it always survives, in the end, the power which ravished it.[34]

'The Helmet', on the other hand, returns us to the nightmare of totalitarianism. With a deceptively simple, ballad-like form, its opening description of helmet and warrior's face fusing to form an anonymous mask is both *imagiste* in its clarity of presentation and horrifying in its human implications:

> The helmet on his head
> Has melted flesh and bone
> And forged a mask instead
> That always is alone.
>
> (*CP* 168)

The dehumanising process brought about by war and Muir's perception of our communal involvement in it are communicated throughout the poem by means of the destabilising and interchanging of pronouns. In the opening line, for example, the warrior is identifiably human with a helmet on *his* head. However, as human face and inanimate metal helmet fuse, pronouns also become neutered. The 'War has rased *its* brow' and 'upon *it*' of the second stanza are equivocal, their antecedents uncertain and the uncertainty increased by the pun in 'rased' and the consequent ambivalence of meaning. By the third stanza, 'its' seems clearly to relate to the vacant 'space-devouring eyes' of the helmet/mask which has taken over from its human occupant, and at this point Muir's 'pass me' brings the speaker into relationship with the horror, as does the 'I' of the following verse with its worried speculation; while in the penultimate stanza the reader too is pulled into the drama with the change to the plural 'we'. Finally, the poem returns full circle to the opening personalisation of the warrior through the pronoun 'he', but this time, instead of the isolated apartness of the first stanza, both the warrior's terror and the speaker/reader's response are indissolubly linked in the apprehension of the mystery of good and evil and our communal involvement in it. Yet, although linked, there is no comforting coming-together as in the experience depicted in the poem 'The Transfiguration' and its companion account of the socialist procession in Muir's novel *Poor Tom*. Coexistent with the sense of speaker, reader and warrior being drawn together in the horror is the

sense of their ultimate isolation, both from each other and from the true
centre and meaning of human life:

> But he can never come home,
> Nor I get to the place
> Where, tame, the terrors roam
> Whose shadows fill his face.
>
> *(CP* 169)

The poem is a fine example of Muir's ability in his later poetry to pursue
a complex philosophical thought in verse which is deceptively simple
and where ambiguity is both an essential element in the 'message' and a
deliberate part of the formal process, not the chance effect of stylistic
immaturity as in some of his early poems.

As in *The Narrow Place* and *The Voyage*, there are a number of personal
poems in this volume. The sonnets 'Love's Remorse' and 'Love in Time's
Despite' are, like the earlier 'The Confirmation', love-poems addressed
to Willa Muir. Yet even they seem to have been conditioned by the
sombre events of Prague in that both return to Muir's early obsession
with Time. In the former, the poet feels 'remorse for all that time has
done / To you, my love'. Both 'the loved and the lover' grow old.
'Eternity alone our wrong can right, / That makes all young again in
time's despite.' 'Love in Time's Despite' concludes on a positive note
in defiance of Time:

> And we who love and love again can dare
> To keep in his despite our summer still,
> Which flowered, but shall not wither, at his will.
>
> *(CP* 181)

Yet the diction and imagery within the poem – 'driven', 'cold
conqueror', 'unfeeling lover', 'robs', 'trampling your tender harvests
over and over' – together with the emphatic rhythms of the final three
lines leading to the final word 'will', leave one with an impression of
willed defiance as opposed to a genuine coming to terms with mortality.

Finally, I wish to comment on 'The Transfiguration' and the Greek-
myth from 'Oedipus'. Muir had attempted the theme of the
Transfiguration as early as *First Poems* in the 'Ballad of the Nightingale',
where the dreaming priest beholds transfigured the 'murderers in red
raiment', harlots robed for bridal' and the beasts who 'lift up their faces /
Like statues, and adore' *(CP* 27). As a young man, he had himself
undergone 'transfiguration' experiences during religious revivalist
meetings and during a socialist May Day procession in Glasgow. He
told a Miss Maisie Spens, who wrote to him about *The Labyrinth*

'Transfiguration' poem, that the Gospel story of Christ's Transfiguration was one which 'filled me with wonder' as a child. 'The idea of Judas going back into innocence has often been with me' (*SL* 148). However, he was apparently unaware when he wrote the poem of its relationship with Christian writings around the theme of the Transfiguration.

Despite his acknowledgement of his early absorption in the Gospel Transfiguration story and his poem's obvious relationship with it, Muir does not commit the poem itself to a specifically Christian interpretation, linking it rather with what he described in his letter to Miss Spens as 'that transmutation of life which is found occasionally in poetry, and in the literature of prophecy, and sometimes in one's own thoughts when they are still' (*SL* 148). As such, it relates more to the Transfiguration experience in the Glasgow May Day procession retold in *Poor Tom*, where

> everything was transfigured: the statues in George Square standing in the sky and fraternally watching them, the vacant buildings, the empty warehouses which they passed when presently they turned into Glassford Street, the rising and falling shoulders, even the pot-bellied, middle-aged man by his side; for all distinction had been lost, all substance transmuted in this transmutation of everything into rhythmical motion and sound. He was not now an isolated human being walking with other isolated human beings from a definite place to a definite place, but part of a perfect rhythm which had arisen, he did not know how. (*PT* 103–4)

In 'The Transfiguration' poem, the experience captured is just such a timeless moment which 'gave back to us the clear unfallen world' (*CP* 185). Everything is transfigured: clothes, animals, refuse heaps, murderers

> And those who hide within the labyrinth
> Of their own loneliness and greatness came,
> And those entangled in their own devices,
> The silent and the garrulous liars, all
> Stepped out of their dungeons and were free.
>   (*CP* 186)

The use of the first person plural pronouns 'we' and 'us' is inclusive, bringing all – poet, reader and poem's characters – into the happening. The tone, however, is not assertive but speculative, and, as in Muir's own experiences of religious conversion and of the May Day procession, and as in his poem 'The Voyage', the vision is transitory: 'the world / Rolled back into its place, and we are here, / And all that radiant kingdom lies forlorn, / As if it had never stirred'. There is, too, less certainty than one might expect to find in a conventional Christian poem. The question 'Was it a vision?' is echoed in the later, hesitant 'But he will come again, it's said' (*CP* 186). Yet despite such lack of assurance – perhaps indeed because of that very lack – the poem in my view succeeds in a way that the assertive depiction of the gods in 'The Labyrinth' does not. The heightened visionary moment and return to reality ring true to human experience in an age of uncertainty and to Muir's own particulr dialectical procedure in his poems of spiritual exploration. His questioning leaves one once again with that sense of the mystery of human life that he found in Hölderlin as opposed to a specific meaning imposed upon it.

In addition, in its relationship with the Glasgow May Day procession, the poem directs us towards the interdependence and communality which were intrinsic both to Muir's socialism and to his Orkney upbringing, but which he had found absent from the communism fashionable among many writers and intellectuals in London in the 1930s. Remembering that 1930s period in *An Autobiography*, he said he

> felt no temptation to become a Communist, for I had been a Socialist in my twenties, when we thought more of humanity and brotherhood than of class-war and revolution. . . . I had been made a Socialist by the degradation of the poor and the hope for an eventual reign of freedom, justice and brotherhood. Instead of these things Communism offered me the victory of a class, and substituted the proletariat for a moral idea. It was as if a conjuring trick had been played with a hope as old as Isaiah, and what the heart had conceived as love and peace had been transmuted into anger and conflict. (*A* 233–4).

His experience of communism in Czechoslovakia increased this sense of a trick played on human aspirations, when loyalty to a system replaced human love, forgiveness and intimations of transfiguration. Such lack of true humanity and spirituality reminded him also of the Scottish Covenanters and their uncompromising religion, their banners displaying the paradoxical slogan: 'Christ and No Quarter'. 'How could one', he asks, 'expect hatred and violence to achieve the ideal community?' (*A* 235–6).

In 'Oedipus', Muir returns to Greek myth to explore the mystery at the heart of human life, together with themes of guilt and innocence and the Calvinist predestination which is a recurring preoccupation in his work. The poem is written in the first person and in a flexible blank-verse form which allows the speaker's thoughts to move freely backwards and forwards as he remembers the events of his past and attempts to find a reason behind the apparently meaningless way imposed upon human action. Oedipus was 'made to stumble', and in the opening lines he seems to accept that he is a man

> Who as in innocent play sought out his guilt,
> And now through guilt seeks other innocence,
> Beset by evil thoughts, led by the gods.
>
> (*CP* 178)

Yet despite this apparent acceptance of his preordained fate and the guilt that seems inseparable from human activity, Oedipus cannot dismiss from his mind and emotions his awareness of the loving relationship he had shared with Jocasta:

> did we sin
> Then on that bed before the light came on us,
> Desiring good to each other, bringing, we thought,
> Great good to each other? But neither guilt nor death.
>
> (*CP* 178)

Here we are confronted not only with the deterministic power of the Greek gods but also with the un-Christlike face of Calvinist Christianity with its disregard of *human* love and worth. Just as the strict Scottish Kirk with its regulations and doctrine of the Elect encouraged a censoriousness which often soured human relations and found evil in innocence, so Oedipus finds that the censoriousness of his gods, who had willed both his guilt and his innocence of the true nature of his actions, now destroys even the memory of his love for Jocasta before the inadmissibility of their relationship was made known to him. Now, instead of loving memories, he finds

> guilt, only guilt, my nostrils choke
> With the smell of guilt, and I can scarcely breathe
> Here in the guiltless guilt-evoking sun.
>
> (*CP* 179)

Muir's exploration of the paradox of guilt and innocence, freedom of action and preordained fate brings him to a point where Oedipus's acceptance of the burden of guilt placed upon him causes him to act out the role of the mythical hero described in Lillian Feder's *Ancient Myth in Modern Poetry*. In Feder's view,

> we identify with the hero of myth not only because he acts out our unconscious wishes and fears but also because in so doing he performs a continual rite of service for the rest of mankind: he asks our essential questions and he answers them. The mythical hero's whole career is devoted to action which raises questions about and

indicates possible answers to those issues we usually avoid: death, our relation to time, destiny, freedom of will. For these answers he pays a price most men do not have the strength or courage to pay.[35]

The depiction of Oedipus in Muir's poem might be thought to raise parallels not only with Feder's mythical hero but also with the Christian story and the sacrifice of the innocent Christ in order to redeem the sins of men. Here, however, the innocent god at the heart of the Christian myth is replaced by an innocent man made guilty by the will of the gods and their control over human actions. Nor does Oedipus, as Christ did, pay his price in order to absolve men of their guilt, but 'that so men's guilt might be made manifest' and 'the immortal burden of the *gods*' eased (*CP* 180; my italics).

Thus, instead of helping to justify and clarify the 'just and irreprehensible but incomprehensible judgment'[36] of the gods (whether Greek or Calvinist), the poem would appear to deepen the mystery of good and evil in human life. In humanist terms, Muir has exalted man in the person of Oedipus as the spokesman and representative of his fellow men and as helpmate of the gods. Yet his sacrifice is, in human terms, negated by the power of the gods who have laid it down that human beings should pay the price for the wrong 'driven deep into our fathomless hearts' by the very gods themselves (*CP* 180). As Muir said of the fatalistic element in the novels of Thomas Hardy, in such a situation 'misfortune is a principle of the universe and falls upon the weak and the strong indiscriminately, neither averted by wisdom nor brought on by folly, striking inevitably and yet as if by chance' (*ELS* 111).

As we have seen in the foregoing discussion and as we shall see also in the *One Foot in Eden* collection, ambivalence and ambiguity can be a positive force in Muir's mature work, a way of preserving the sense of mystery with regard to human life. Yet, however compelling 'Oedipus' is as a poem – and it is one which I find myself returning to again and again – philosophically its ambiguity is ultimately destructive, focusing attention on the impossibility of human self-determination in such a restrictive, preordained world. For a more satisfying philosophical assessment of the forces of good and evil in human life and the operation of human freedom within a context of uncertain and restrictive fate, one has to await the insights of Muir's final volume, *One Foot in Eden*.

NOTES

1. Neil M. Gunn, Review of *The Narrow Place*, *Scots Magazine* XXXIX, no 2, May 1943, p. 163.

2. Neil M. Gunn, 'Scott and Scotland by Edwin Muir', *Scots Magazine* XXVI, no 1, October 1936, p. 73.

3. Butter, *Man and Poet*, p. 178.

4. Huberman, *The Field of Good and Ill*, pp. 107, 106, 134.

5. Willa Muir, letter of 17 November 1966 to Ernest and Janette Marwick, Orkney Archives D31/31/6.

6. Edwin Muir, quoted in Butter, *Man and Poet*, pp. 167–8.

7. See P. H. Butter (ed.), *Complete Poems of Edwin Muir* (Aberdeen: Association for Scottish Literary Studies, 1991), p. 330.

8. See Butter, *Man and Poet*, pp. 204–5.

9. T. S. Eliot, 'Burnt Norton', *Four Quartets*, p. 14.

10. Hugh MacDiarmid, *A Drunk Man Looks at the Thistle, Complete Poems*, p. 143.

11. Muir, 'Chapbook', BBC Radio, 3 September 1952, quoted in Butter, *Man and Poet*, p. 206.

12. Muir, 'Chapbook', BBC Radio, 3 September 1952. Quoted in Butter, *Man and Poet*, pp. 215–16.

13. Butter, *Man and Poet*, p. 216.

14. Hölderlin, 'Hyperions Schiksaalslied', *Harrap Anthology*, p. 2.

15. Muir, quoted in Butter, *Man and Poet*, pp. 215–16.

16. Butter, *Man and Poet*, p. 216.

17. Wiseman, *Beyond the Labyrinth*, pp. 64, 63.

18. Huberman, *The Field of Good and Ill*, p. 167.

19. MacDiarmid, *In Memoriam James Joyce, Complete Poems*, p. 840.

20. Kathleen Raine, 'Edwin Muir: An Appreciation', *Texas Quarterly* IV, no 3, Autumn 1961, p. 242.

21. Elizabeth Jennings, 'Edwin Muir as Poet and Allegorist,' *London Magazine* 7, no 3, March 1960, p. 54.

22. Butter, *Man and Poet*, p. 222.

23. James Aitchison, *The Golden Harvester: The Vision of Edwin Muir* (Aberdeen: Aberdeen University Press, 1988), p. 152.

24. Huberman, *The Field of Good and Ill*, p. 168.

25. Wiseman, *Beyond the Labyrinth*, p. 75.

26. Rainer Maria Rilke, *Duino Elegies*, translated by J. B. Leishman and Stephen Spender (London: Hogarth Press, 1939), fourth revised edition (Chatto & Windus, 1963), pp. 44–5.

27. Wiseman, *Beyond the Labyrinth*, pp. 77, 83.

28. Huberman, *The Field of Good and Ill*, p. 168.

29. Karl Kraus, quoted in 'Satirist in the Modern World', unsigned article in *The Times Literary Supplement*, 8 May 1953, p. 295.

30. Edwin Morgan, 'Edwin Muir', *Essays* (Cheadle Hume: Carcanet, 1974), pp. 188–9.

31. Muir, quoted in Butter, *Man and Poet*, p. 223.

32. William Wordsworth, *The Prelude* (1805) (London: Oxford University Press, 1933), paperback ed. (1970), p. 11.

33. Edwin Muir, 'Bolshevism and Calvinism', *European Quarterly*, May 1934, pp. 9, 7, 4.

34. Václav Havel, 'Letter to Dr Gustáv Husák' (1975), *Living in Truth*, ed. Jan Vladislav (London: Faber & Faber, 1987), p. 27.

35. Feder, *Ancient Myth in Modern Poetry*, pp. 11–12.

36. John Calvin, *Institutes of the Christian Religion*, quoted by Karl K. Dannenfeldt in *The Church of the Renaissance and Reformation* (St Louis and London: Concordia Publishing House, 1970), p. 134.

Four

Criticism and the Poetic Imagination

As in his poetry, Muir as critic stands apart from the mainstream of criticism in this century. His writing is animated by the tradition of Renaissance humanism, with its emphasis on the imagination and on the moral purpose of art – to teach by delighting – rather than by the formalist, analytical approaches more characteristic of this century's work in criticism. For Muir, such a concentration on the formal aspects of a work of art destroyed its essential unity and the potentiality for communication. As he wryly observed in relation to the methods of New Criticism: 'it gives me a faint touch of claustrophobia, the feeling that I am being confined in a narrow place with the poem and the critic, and that I shall not get away until all three of us are exhausted' (*EP* 69). He was troubled by the contemporary concentration on formal analysis, believing it a loss to literature which left 'the work of intermediation . . . to critics of less contemporary repute' (*EP* 61–2). He saw literature as having a freeing, emancipating role, such as he himself had experienced through contact with the *New Age*, and he looked to nineteenth-century writers such as Arnold and the English and German Romantics as exemplars of this tradition.

Among noteworthy aspects of Muir's critical writing, therefore, are this avoidance of formal analysis and an affinity with the nineteenth-century context, in particular with the poet and critic Matthew Arnold. On the other hand, Muir was not merely a conservative critic who felt more at home with the traditional approaches of a previous century than he did with the analytical methods of his own. He was genuinely and contemporaneously working through the accidents of his own life and through a clash of cultures more usually associated with an earlier period, and it is this first-hand personal experience of culture shock which gives his mature criticism its enduring strength, despite his hostility to formal analysis, and which positions him firmly in the tradition of humanist criticism.

As we have seen, Muir's first collection of criticism was *We Moderns*, a miscellany of aphorisms heavily influenced by Nietzsche. In later years, he was at pains to reject the book and its Nietzschean assertiveness, yet one can recognise in sections such as 'Creative Love' and 'The Tragic View' the need which Nietzsche supplied for Muir at this time: a philosophy which appeared to offer a context in which his family tragedies could be reconciled. Nietzsche taught him that the living moment 'is what it is' by virtue of one's past experiences: 'justify it and you justify them . . . the years which you lived altogether bereft of hope . . . all these are unconsciously affirmed in your affirmation of this moment. Let them be affirmed consciously!' (*WM* 229). On the other hand, alongside the uncharacteristic poses are philosophical positions more typical of Muir. Several sections demonstrate his recurring preoccupation with Original Sin and the Fall of Man. His statement that 'the advanced have made up their minds about all the problems of existence but not about the problem of existence' (*WM* 13) anticipates his later criticism of contemporary fiction-writers such as Huxley. As Arnold had earlier rejected Clough's plea for topicality, Muir here insists that the 'eternal problem' of the ancients should be the matter of art, not the 'reproduction' of life of the modern realists, the desire for drama about ' "the marriage question", or bad housing, or the Labour Party' (*WM* 15–16).

We Moderns was followed in the *New Age* by a series of still uncollected social criticism articles, 'Our Generation', in which the influence of Nietzsche again predominates. Concurrent with this influence, however, is Muir's recurring vision of culture as emancipation, a self-freeing and developing process. Ritchie Robertson has pointed to Muir's sense of alienation in London when he was writing these 'Our Generation' articles and to the obstacles to emancipation which he found in the metropolitan environment.[1] It is interesting, on the other hand, to compare Muir's account with Catherine Carswell's depiction of provincial Glasgow bourgeois life in her novels *Open the Door!* (1920) and *The Camomile* (1922) and also with his own autobiographical novel, *Poor Tom*, set in Glasgow. Similarities suggest that in this cultural emancipation context, as in so much else, Muir's principal source of frustration was not the metropolis but the Glasgow of the early years of this century.

Muir's critical reputation developed during the 1920s through his continuing periodical reviewing and three more critical books: two collections of essays, *Latitudes* (1924) and *Transition* (1926), and the *Structure of the Novel*, a more expansive consideration of fictional form.

Latitudes consists principally of reviews and essays written for the *Freeman* journal between 1921 and 1923 and continues to demonstrate the Nietzschean assertiveness of *We Moderns*. Muir himself later dismissed it as 'nonsense combined with overweening confidence' (*SL* 203–4) and found little in it worth reprinting. It does, nevertheless, exhibit his eclectic interests and in particular his interest in European writers, a legacy from his involvement with the *New Age*. *Transition* is less typical of Muir in that it concentrates exclusively on English-language literary figures, chief among whom are James Joyce, D. H. Lawrence, Virginia Woolf and T. S. Eliot.

It is at this stage in Muir's career that one becomes aware of the negative effects of his lack of interest in analytical critical methodology. While in later essays on literature and society a philosophical approach would be in keeping with the development of his themes, in *Transition* and in other interwar period review essays on contemporary literature he often seems at a loss for the appropriate analytical tools, focusing primarily on what seems to be the 'message' of the text and ignoring perspectives brought about by innovative structuring and techniques. This can lead him to make what in retrospect seem strange judgments in regard to early twentieth-century writers. He admired Eliot the critic, and his *Latitudes* essay 'A Plea for Psychology in Literary Criticism', first published in the *Athenaeum* in January 1921, shows the influence of Eliot's 'Tradition and the Individual Talent' (1919) in its insistence on the impersonality of art and the rejection of biographical criticism: 'for this task of illumination, the works of a writer are all that is required; anything outside them, indeed, is irrelevant' (*L* 100) – a paradoxical position for someone with Muir's hostility to New Criticism methodology. As one might expect, Eliot the poet was not so favoured. Like Huxley's fiction, Eliot's poetry 'expresses an attitude to life, not a principle of life . . . As a poet Mr Eliot lacks seriousness [and is] till now a poet of inferior range' (*T* 140–1, 144). D. H. Lawrence provoked even more hostility, Muir's response being at best equivocal, at worst derogatory and dismissive. Both *We Moderns* and *Latitudes* attacked Lawrence and the kind of literature he represented as 'nihilistic' and its popularity as pointing 'to a disintegration of personality which must be general' (*L* 174). *Latitudes* also linked Lawrence's writings on sex with Freudian psychoanalysis and found both 'filthy' (*L* 178–9), while the *Scottish Nation* article 'The Assault on Humanism' (1923) found Lawrence the chief instigator of a philosophy which Muir considered was attacking the foundations of humanist morality. *Transition* attempts to give a more balanced account of Lawrence's work, drawing attention to his 'most obviously striking quality . . . a kind of splendour, not of the spirit, nor of the mind, but of the senses and instincts' (*T* 49). Lawrence, however, has 'never drawn a complete character' (*T* 57). It does not seem to have occurred to Muir that 'the old, stable ego of the character',[2] as Lawrence described it, might not be Lawrence's objective and that an innovative literary style and a preoccupation with states of being and feeling might work together to explore and define less conscious dimensions of 'life as we know it' (*T* 50).

Muir's most positive comments in these early critical writings are reserved for James Joyce and Virginia Woolf. His *Transition* essay on Joyce appeared in several periodicals in the 1920s and was reproduced with minor omissions in *James Joyce: The Critical Heritage*, edited by Robert Deming in 1970. In his praise of Joyce, he rejects the earlier impersonality theory put forward in *Latitudes*, finding, more characteristically, 'a necessary and an organic relation between him and his work, to create being, as Ibsen said, an act of emancipation' (*T* 23). What interests Muir, however, is not the formal metaphorical structuring of *Ulysses* or its overt stylistic features, but rather the fact that it seems to come out of a 'folk rather than a literary inspiration'. He finds, for example, that the prostitutes in Nighttown are 'figures in a folk-lore which mankind continually creates, or rather carries with it . . . the aesthetic utterance of the illiterate classes and of the illiterate parts of our nature, which co-exists with literature, but in a separate world'. This voice 'is not inarticulate; but it expresses itself anonymously' (*T* 33). It is therefore this mythical quality in Joyce which speaks to Muir, the mythical quality which drew him also to Greek myth and inspired his lasting involvement with the Scottish ballads, a world in which was to be found 'the roots of poetry, where we should all be' (*SL* 185). And in relation to what he sees as the isolation of the artist in the modern world, he finds that 'Mrs Woolf alone, perhaps, has kept intact her sense of the reality of communication' (*T* 215).

The Structure of the Novel is a unique item in Muir's output, being an expansive critical analysis of a popular literary form as opposed to the short and necessary partial reviews of individual writers and works which he wrote for periodicals and included in his collections of criticism. Published in 1928, it must have been written during the period between *The Marionette* and *The Three Brothers* when he was preoccupied with the novel both as novelist himself and as translator. Its significance and lasting popularity can be seen in the number of reprints which it has attracted.

For Muir, 'structure' equals 'plot', and the book is principally concerned with the different kind of plots or actions which have developed in the novel since its inception in the eighteenth century. He isolates three principal structures (with subsets, or 'off-shoots', as he categorises the experimental fiction of Henry James, which he did not appreciate): the novel of character, the dramatic novel and the chronicle novel. Of these three, Muir's interest is primarily in the dramatic novel with its causal action and character development. Here, he finds 'fate' working within the lives of the characters as opposed to operating externally to them.

The heart of Muir's book is the chapter 'Time and Space'. For him, Time in the novel is not a literary tool, a device for structuring the narrative through the temporal allocation of past, present and future actions; nor is it the kind of anachronistic interweaving of time isolated by Genette in his analysis of Proust's *A la recherche du temps perdu*, a novel which features prominently in Muir's account of contemporary fiction. For Muir, Time is *philosophical* time, and the dramatic novel with its psychological and causally-propelled action is significant not because of its underlying structural patterns but because, through its actions, we are enabled to know more about human motivation and the nature of human life. Human beings may fail in such a novel; there is no guarantee of a happy ending as there most often is in a romance or character novel. Yet human beings are not helpless spectators or victims of a fate which they cannot understand or attempt to control. They are players in their own lives – an emphasis which may well be related to the similar search for understanding and integration in his own life that we have seen in his early poetry and in his novels. It is interesting to note how often the word 'fate' and a preoccupation with determinism occurs in the discourse of the study. At one point, indeed, Muir appears to anticipate possible criticism:

> In introducing, to some it will appear irrelevantly, the concepts of Time, Space and Causality into a work of criticism, I may appear to have forgotten all the aesthetic canons, and to be erecting arbitrary and fanciful standards . . . the only reply I can make is that in trying to find the reasons for the apparently arbitrary limitations of certain forms of the novel, I was driven back at last to the limitations of our vision of the world. (*SN* 113)

In view of his unwillingness to investigate, or sometimes even to recognise as valid, experimental modernist techniques in literature, it is surprising to find Muir so consistent in his championing of three writers whom we now consider to have been in the vanguard of early twentieth-century innovation: Joyce, Virginia Woolf and Proust. Joyce and Woolf feature prominently and positively in *Transition* and in *The Structure of the Novel*, and Joyce's *Ulysses* and Proust's *A la recherche du temps perdu* are discussed in the latter as 'the two outstanding works of prose fiction of the present age' (*SN* 124). Yet neither fits happily into Muir's defined structural categories and neither conforms to the kind of ordered pattern that he looked for in a work of fiction. Somewhat confusingly for the reader, after his eulogistic introduction of Joyce, his account of *Ulysses* reads more like a catalogue of its faults than an indication of its positive qualities: 'its design is arbitrary, its development feeble, its unity questionable. . . . The symbolism . . . is hardly to be taken seriously' (*SN* 227). The *Ulysses* plot, in fact, 'is simply a framework intended to keep the story's formlessness within bounds, an external mould to prevent the theme from running into complete chaos' (*SN* 128).

Just as, in his autobiography, Muir was to describe his relations with his psychoanalyst as his conscious mind putting up a fight while his 'unconscious, like a treacherous spy, was enthusiastically working for the analyst' (*A* 158), so, in reading Muir's criticism of certain early twentieth-century poetry and fiction, one senses that his intuitive imaginative response is reaching out to the work while his conscious, traditional, humanist critical criteria are insisting that twentieth-century art has taken a wrong turning. Thus he was one of the first and most perceptive critics to comment on Hugh MacDiarmid's modernist Scots lyrics of the early 1920s and on his long, innovative dramatic monologue, *A Drunk Man Looks at the Thistle*. His account of Joyce's 'faults' is in reality a perceptive comment on the elliptical juxtaposition-ing found in much modernist art, music and literature:

> Mr Joyce uses no transitions at all; he paints a solid block of his canvas, and when it is done goes on to another. The result is . . . a succession of parts, done in different styles, making up a whole which is loose and redundant, but *not unimpressive* [my italics]. (*SN* 128–9).

What attracted Muir to Joyce, Woolf and Proust, despite his conscious rejection of the formal techniques in their fiction, was what he saw as the philosophical context of their work. He saw all three as preoccupied with philosophical time and human mortality, with a search for self-knowledge and self-determination. Unlike Lawrence, who stood at the opposite pole of modernism to Joyce, these fiction-writers seemed to Muir to be able to impose a classical patterning on the muddle of living experience as opposed to revelling in the disorder as Lawrence seemed to him to do. It did not seem to occur to him – or perhaps he did not allow it to occur to him – that the fragmentary, disordered, at times nihilistic forms of art found in the early twentieth century offered a more reliable picture of life in our times than could be achieved through the imposed artistic criteria and patterns of a bygone age. Muir's own battle with chaos was perhaps at this period still too fragile in its outcome for him to allow himself to respond without reserve to the more extreme art forms of his time.

During the 1930s, Muir became more involved with Scottish culture, and his book-length criticism at that period is primarily on Scottish matters. His one English literature critical book is *The Present Age* (1939) in the *Introductions to English Literature* series under the general editorship of Bonamy Dobrée, but he was unhappy with it and asked that it should not be reprinted with the rest of the series. Its principal fault seems to me to lie in its structure, which, unlike the more expansive *Structure of the Novel*, follows the short essay format of his periodical-reviewing and so is unable to give an overview of the period or to distinguish between major and minor trends. It does also, however, demonstrate his continuing uncertainty when faced with the contradictory stylistic and philosophical attitudes of the modern period.

Muir's most mature collections of critical writings are *Essays on Literature and Society* (1949) and *The Estate of Poetry*, a series of lectures given at Harvard University between 1955 and 1956 in which he examined the relationship between the poet and his public. As we have seen, 1949 was the year also of *The Labyrinth*, and the essays in part derive from the theme of the single, disunited world which was increasingly preoccupying Muir. They deal with literature and society not as discrete entities but contextually, something which was always implicitly present in Muir's critical method but which is now given more overt definition.

Essays on Literature and Society opens with 'Robert Henryson', Muir's elegiac tribute to the lost philosophical coherence of a past age and an essay which sets the course for the book as a whole with its dominant theme of the search for wholeness in the modern world. Muir points to the age of Henryson as one of 'settlement, religious, intellectual and social [where] an agreement had been reached regarding the nature and meaning of human life, and the imagination could attain harmony and tranquillity' (*ELS* 10). This is not, however, a nostalgic essay. Nor is it the kind of wish for escape or security suggested by Tennyson's late *Idylls* or Hopkins's movement towards a 'Heaven, Haven' in his early poetry. Muir does not deny the 'practical disorder' of life in this medieval age of faith, but what for him gives it its coherence and philosophical stability is that this disorder in everyday earthly life and the tragedies which inevitably accompanied it were seen 'as part of a greater story about which there is general consent', the virtue of which 'while it lasted was that it made everything natural, even tragedy; so that while pity had a place, there was no place for those outcries against life which fill the tragic drama of the next age' (*ELS* 10). He finds that

Henryson's poetry is animated by this sense of being 'part of a greater story' and that the communication of this sense is 'strong enough still, in spite of all that has happened since, to produce a composing effect on us'. Nevertheless, as in the poetry of *The Labyrinth*, there is no going back. 'It is the virtue of an age, not ours, and it required to embody it a particular form of art, not ours' (*ELS* 11).

This essay and 'The Politics of *King Lear*' show Muir's approach to criticism at its best. The *King Lear* essay was first given at Glasgow University as the W. P. Ker Lecture for 1946 and Muir is at pains to make it clear that he himself is not a professional scholar in the traditional academic sense but someone who has 'come to books when I could, in the intervals of a life spent on other things, many of them not of my choosing' (*ELS* 33). Yet, despite this disarming modesty, Muir's experience is of a kind which he has always believed essential for the production and interpretation of literature which cannot, in his view, be the product of an Axel's Castle existence. The critic, and by implication the artist also, must

> bring to his interpretation of works of imagination not only his reading, but his life, the experiences he has passed through, the emotions he has felt, the reflections he has made upon them, even the accidents and trivialities of every day, since they are all part of life and help us, therefore, to comprehend the poet's image of life. (*ELS* 33)

This in effect is Muir's poetic and critical credo, and its inclusions and exclusions prefigure the strengths and weaknesses of his critical approach.

As in the Henryson essay, Muir now applies this view of the essential relationship between literature and society to Shakespeare's *King Lear*, which he sees as a tragedy arising from an age of transition where individualism and competition have taken over from the communal traditions of the medieval world and where two conflicting and irreconcilable ideologies confront each other. In this interpretation of *King Lear*, Muir anticipates the approach of John Danby in his 1949 study of the play *Shakespeare's Doctrine of Nature*, [3] but, while Danby's interpretation is now part of the critical canon in Shakespeare studies, Muir's essay would appear to be less well known. Danby saw the play in terms of conflicting theories of Nature held in Shakespeare's time, a reading which, as in Muir's 1946 lecture, puts the emphasis on ideological interpretation as opposed to the individual character studies of earlier Shakespearean critics such as Bradley. For Muir and Danby, Lear represents an older order of society, perhaps that communal world from which Chaucer's and Henryson's poetry evolved, 'an order of

society so obviously springing from the nature and needs of man'
(*ELS* 46); while Goneril, Regan, Cornwall and Edmund are the new
generation who have quite a different concept of 'natural' obligations, a
concept which would be formulated by Hobbes in his *Leviathan* (1651),
but one which had been developing throughout the sixteenth century
and would have been familiar to educated Elizabethans through the
plays of Chapman and Marlowe and what Muir calls the Realpolitik of
Machiavelli's *The Prince*. 'They are quite rational, but only on the lowest
plane of reason, and they have that contempt for other ways of thinking
which comes from a knowledge of their own efficiency' (*ELS* 40). They
live in 'a continuous present divested of all associations, denuded of
memory and the depth which memory gives to life' (*ELS* 43). This is
Muir's concept of the 'new man', the Usurpers of his *Labyrinth* poem of
that name, and, in the place of traditional relationships which embrace
both the care of the individual and the stability of the family and
community, this new man offers an adversarial ideology which
embodies competition and suspicion.

   One of the interesting aspects of Muir's reading of *King Lear*,
therefore, and one which contributes to its conviction and strength, is
his perception of what one might call (although he himself would be
unlikely to do so) the Marxian dialectic of this confrontation and its
place in the recurring evolutionary pattern of human life. In addition,
although as a rule he was unsympathetic to theoretical or formal
criticism, Muir's perception of the twentieth-century relevance of the
play comes close to postmodernist perspectives on the untying of a text
and its capacity to say what it did not initially appear to say or was not
intended to say. Muir comments: 'The play contains, therefore, or has
taken on, a significance which Shakespeare probably could not have
known, and without his being aware, he wrote in it the mythical drama
of the transmutation of civilisation' (*ELS* 35). In this account of
Shakespeare's achievement in *King Lear*, Muir may be giving voice to his
recurrent view that the most significant kind of poetry has this capacity
for universality and allegorical interpretation, but he is also no less
surely putting his finger on that silence in a text which can become a
voice for succeeding generations, a latent potentiality which, while not
destroying its recognisable identity, can allow it to be continually
reinterpreted. Muir saw the applicability of Lear's struggle to the
confrontation with fascism which had erupted in a second world war and
with the communism which now threatened the achievement of postwar
stability in Europe. As we have seen in the discussion of *The Labyrinth*
poems, his 1946 lecture did in reality anticipate his experience in
postwar Prague where the usurping communists re-enacted the drama of

Shakespeare's conflicting ideologies, a drama in which – in Albany's words – 'humanity must perforce prey on itself / Like monsters of the deep' (IV ii 48–9).

In addition to the essays on Henryson and *King Lear* and the closing essays on poetry and the poetic imagination added to the revised edition, some of the best essays in the collection concern the European writers Hölderlin and Kafka, together with an assessment of the determinist philosophy of Thomas Hardy's novels. There are two essays on Hölderlin, of which one is general and the other is on his *Patmos* poem. In both, as in the essay on Kafka, one is aware of the relationship with the philosophical context of Muir's own poetry. These Hölderlin essays, first published in the 1930s, are more specific than the 1923 *Scottish Nation* essay on the German poet.[4] In the later essays, Muir points to the interaction between the human world and the world of Hölderlin's gods, 'the recurring effect of passing at one step from the world of time and change to that of timelessness, and back again' – evidence for him that 'time and timelessness are inextricably bound up' (*ELS* 88–90). Like Muir himself, Hölderlin 'approached the mystery of time and eternity through the imagination . . . the mystery itself, not any particular manifestation of it, was his theme; and what he made out of it was a mythology' (*ELS* 103).

The essay on Kafka is especially relevant to the themes of Muir's poetry, which was preoccupied with the metaphor of 'the way' before he discovered Kafka's work as reader or translator. He says:

> The image of a road comes into our minds when we think of his stories; for in spite of all the confusions and contradictions in which he was involved he held that life was a way, not a chaos, that the right way exists and can be found by a supreme and exhausting effort. (*ELS* 121)

In addition, the sense of our common destiny which was so important for Muir is to be found in Kafka also: 'The hero of the two great stories is anybody, and his story is the story of anybody' (*ELS* 124). We have here an instance of Muir's intuitive response to a work of art which speaks to him of an underlying belief that life has meaning despite its anarchic surface, and he communicates the sureness of that response. Yet, as we have found in his admiration of Joyce, Proust and Woolf, Muir here ignores the markers of *impasse* and uncertainty which Kafka's works also contain, but which he would appear to believe are secondary to its deeper significance.

Thomas Hardy's fiction also spoke to Muir at a deep level, but whereas Muir perceived in Kafka's novels an intimation of a 'right way' despite the deceitful roads one must travel in the search for it, in

Hardy's novels he found that 'misfortune is not brought about by men and women, but is arranged by this power which is indifferent to all arrangements and therefore to misfortune itself'. Misfortune is therefore 'a principle of the universe' (*ELS* 111), and the lawmaker of the universe appears something akin to the iron god of Calvinism. It is therefore in the depiction of endurance that Muir finds Hardy's strength as novelist, for, as he himself dramatised in the poem 'The Combat', 'by enduring man seems to rise above the malice of fate by a pure act of magnanimity comprehensible only to himself' (*ELS* 119).

In his Harvard lectures for 1955–6, published posthumously in 1962, and in the final two essays added to the revised edition of *Essays on Literature and Society*, Muir returns overtly to the question of the relationship between literature and society. In addition, 'A View of Poetry' reviews the situation of poetry in the early years of this century and his own previous negative response to it. As Stephen Spender had argued in 'Literature and Public Events' in response to Muir's condemnation of modernist writing in 'The Natural Man and the Political Man', Muir now accepts that

> for the good of its future, if it was to have one, poetry had to submit to a phase of almost surgical experiment . . . for the style of poetry now and then tends to harden until poets can no longer say what they want to say, and new styles have to be found to enable them to speak freely. (*ELS* 228)

Yet the negative resonances of his phrase 'phase of almost surgical experiment' suggest his still grudging attitude towards early twentieth-century experimentation in the arts. He continues to be unenthusiastic about analytical criticism and what he considers to be the convention of obscurity which has developed in its wake. While he is prepared to accept that Eliot's early poetry was necessarily difficult because of its revolutionary nature, he finds that thereafter 'criticism went on to conclude that all poetry is difficult, a thing to be enquired into, as if it were a scientific problem'. It is here that we find the condemnation, repeated in his Harvard lectures, that to participate in New Criticism is 'to be shut in with the critic and the poem . . . knowing that I shall not get away until all three of us are exhausted' (*ELS* 231–2).

Muir's belief is that 'the animating spirit of poetry is imagination, and the work of the imagination is to seize life as it lives and moves, in its individuality' (*ELS* 232–3). While the scientific and analytic mind has increasingly dominated thought in the modern world, he believes that it is only through imagination that we can see this modern world 'rooted in a past whose extent we cannot measure, and perhaps never will be able to measure. Imagination unites us with humanity in time and space . . . and our lives would not have any meaning if they were quite without it' (*ELS* 234). This is the theme also of 'The Poetic Imagination', where Muir points to the difference between the scientific and poetic imagination and the difference between a scientific and technological world where progress is the keynote, where new machines continually supplant and surpass the old, and the world of human beings where we all have to 'pass through the same ancestral pattern and have the same feelings, the same difficulties as generations long before he was born'. Yet it is this unchanging human world from which the poetic imagination springs, and it is this pattern of 'continuity ruled by repetition' which enables the 'great figures in imaginative literature' to be 'perpetually contemporary' (*ELS* 226, 217).

In *The Estate of Poetry*, Muir confronts the problem of the relationship between contemporary poet and public. Analogous to his view that the poetic imagination is being increasingly undervalued as a result of the dominance of scientific and technological methodology and achievement, he finds that the traditional relationship between poet and readers has been replaced by 'an alarming, vast, shapeless something, deaf and blind to a once recognized and accepted part of life, and a human inheritance'. This new audience is 'the public' (*EP* 2). As Edward Marsh in 1912 saw himself as editing the Georgian Poetry anthologies for busy people who no longer had sufficient leisure to choose for themselves, so Muir accepts, though with protest, that the speeding-up of everyday life 'has forced on us a new kind of sensibility, imposed new habits and with that new ways of thought' which 'are bound to affect our response to literature. Indeed, they may help to explain why we neglect it; we live at such a speed that we are carried right past it' (*EP* 4). He quotes from Wordsworth's 'Preface' to *Lyrical Ballads* in support of his contemporary view of the deadening effects on the imagination of technological and social developments, but he no longer has the nineteenth-century poet's confidence that 'the time is approaching when the evil will be systematically opposed'. Now poetry has become 'a thing which is written for the few, while the mass of the people now read the news and go to the cinema, or sit before a television set' (*EP* 6–7).

As in his previous delineation of the positive relationship between poetry and society in the medieval world, so here Muir is at pains to make it clear that he is not 'advocating a return to a past that has gone forever, or romanticizing the coarseness of peasant life, or its poverty and hardship' (*E* 8). Whatever the material gains which industrialisation and mechanisation have brought, however, he believes that they have been accompanied by a loss of the first-hand experience of living that produced the ballads and their singers and audience:

This artificial world which we have made out of the world, the monotony of the work which produces it, the abundance of the distractions which vainly try to make up for that monotony – all these things, it seems to me, help to explain the depressed state of poetry, and the present neglect of it. (*EP* 9)

Writing at the midpoint of the century and at a time when Europe was still struggling to recover from the Second World War and when television was still a novelty, Muir may have been unduly pessimistic about the decline of poetry – and one might expand his poetry category to include other forms of imaginative literature, visual art and music. He himself unwittingly points to a possible way out of the dilemma in his emphasis on the diversity of human experience. It is true that the contemporary artist can no longer be sure of his or her public in the way that the artist of the past could be sure of a small but similarly-educated and cohesive audience; or in the way that the ballad-singer could be sure of shared popular experience. Our world has become too open and diverse for traditional concepts of 'universality' to remain viable. Diverse subject matter, forms and artistic objectives are matched by equally diverse readers, viewers and listeners with varying experiences and expectations. Yet there is still a sense in which Muir's ideal of communality retains its force. For as he recognised, it is our imaginations which enable us to enter into experiences which are foreign to us, to make the leap into the work of art and play our part in its re-creation. In the last decade of the century, there is little sign that science and technology have permanently damaged the poetic or creative imagination, although they may have given it some hard knocks along the way. Film and television have the potentiality of soporifics, but they have also opened up new worlds for the imagination to play in. New methods in book-production, the expansion of opportunities in performance arts and in visual art exhibitions, and new writings from Africa, Asia, Black America, Australia and from all over the globe present the imagination with a diversity of experience previously unimaginable.

This means, however, that our definitions of 'art' and our view of the traditional relationship between artist and audience may have to be revised. As Eliot in 'Tradition and the Individual Talent' saw the new work of art changing our view of what had gone before, so the diversity of art experiences available to us today must similarly affect our view of the art of past and present and of how audience and artist relate to each other. Artists may no longer be appealing to the one, homogeneous audience, but diversity itself suggests that an audience of some kind is there to be found. In addition, there is a sense that the tide of theorising which took charge of criticism in the postwar period may be ebbing and that it has left in its wake a much more inclusive idea of the work of art than was the case with the specialised, elitist theories of the modernist period. The critic as intermediary may again have a place in the disseminating of new artistic attitudes and evaluations, and art and life may once again be moving closer to each other. This suggests that, at the end of the twentieth century, Muir's humanist stance may be found increasingly relevant.

Muir's definition of imagination is a generous and popular one, extending even to 'gossip', which 'involves invention and . . . is a perpetual reminder that common men are subject to the same pleasures and griefs and the same absurd chances as the great' (*EP* 80). It is therefore a quality which is intrinsic to human life and in its higher forms essential to the production and reception of art. Muir's strength as a critic lies in his situation in this inclusive tradition, in his insistence that art and society are interrelated and that it is through the poetic imagination that we comprehend both art and our common humanity. *The Estate of Poetry*, together with these late essays on literature and society, recalls the poet and artist from the periphery of human activity to a central role in human affairs.

NOTES

1. Ritchie Robertson, '"Our Generation": Edwin Muir as a Social Critic 1920–22', *Scottish Literary Journal* 9 (1982) ii, pp. 45–65.
2. D. H. Lawrence, Letter to Edward Garnet, 5 June 1914, *Letters of D. H. Lawrence*, ed. Aldous Huxley (London: Heinemann, 1932), p. 198.
3. John F. Danby, *Shakespeare's Doctrine of Nature: A Study of King Lear* (1949) (London: Faber & Faber, 1968).
4. For a detailed discussion of the publication history of Muir's Hölderlin essays and of his understanding of the German poet, see P. H. Gaskill, 'Edwin Muir as a Critic of Hölderlin', *Forum for Modern Language Studies* 14 (1978), pp. 345–64.

Five

'My Second Country': Edwin Muir and Scotland

Muir's relationship with Scotland was always an equivocal one. In the 1920s, he held back from full involvement with MacDiarmid's literary renaissance movement 'because after all I'm not Scotch, I'm an Orkney man, a good Scandinavian, and my true country is Norway, or Denmark, or Iceland, or some place like that' (*SL* 64). The 1930s saw him at one time proclaiming his belief in Scottish nationhood and independence because 'I believe that men are capable of organizing themselves only in relatively small communities' and, in contradiction of his earlier position, because 'I am a Scotsman' (*SF* 260); at another writing the controversial *Scott and Scotland* which insisted that the only way forward for Scottish writers was to adopt the English language and absorb the English tradition. In *The Story and the Fable*, he remembered the friendliness with which the playwright Karl Čapek was acknowledged by the people of Prague and commented that 'this warm, easygoing contact could only have been possible in a comparatively small town, and it was the first thing that made me wish that Edinburgh might become a similar place and that Scotland might become a nation again' (*SF* 228). However, his own experience in St Andrews between 1935 and 1942 was an unhappy one, while his final period of residence in Scotland as Warden of Newbattle Abbey College from 1950 to 1955 was clouded by disagreements over policy and factional intrigue. Significantly, the wish 'that Scotland might become a nation again' was excised from the revised version of the auto-biography published in 1954.

Muir's prose writings about Scotland are to be found principally in the articles and reviews written in the 1930s for periodicals such as the *Modern Scot* (and its successor *Outlook*), the London *Bookman* and *Spectator* and in the books *Scottish Journey* (1935) and *Scott and Scotland* (1936). Muir's reviewing took place in a context of an upsurge of literary and political activity in Scotland itself and a corresponding new awareness of the Scottish dimension in London circles. In the early 1930s, for example, *The Spectator* announced an editorial policy of regular coverage of Scottish matters because 'the cultivation of Gaelic and the conscious development of a modern Scottish literature are movements demanding not only observation but discussion'.[1] In addition to articles on Scottish writers of the past such as Sir Walter Scott and Robert Louis Stevenson, for which there was an established interested readership, this reviewing also gave Muir the opportunity, if a regrettably limited one, to introduce and comment on a new generation of Scottish writers such as Hugh MacDiarmid, Lewis Grassic Gibbon, Neil M. Gunn and Fionn MacColla. In his 1934 review of Gibbon's *Grey Granite* in *The Listener*, he runs counter to more recent evaluations of *A Scots Quair*, finding this third book with its urban setting the most successful of the trilogy and thus foregrounding its genesis in the years of the Depression. 'The industrial town of Duncairn, with its strikers and unemployed workmen, is described so vividly that one can see and smell it . . . the account of the beating up of young Ewan Tavendale by the police is extremely powerful.' On the other hand, he complains about the 'preferential treatment' meted out in the earlier books to Chris Guthrie, Gibbon's heroine, and a heroine who has since become mythologised as 'Chris Caledonia' in accounts of Scottish Renaissance fiction. For Muir, however, Chris is 'a picture of what the author wished woman to be, not a picture of a woman'. Similarly in *Grey Granite*, he finds that 'when the author conducts his heroine at the end to the scenes of her childhood and leaves her there, one feels again that he is describing what he wishes to be, not what would be. One cannot take such a thing seriously.'[2] There is little sentimentality here with regard to Scotland's history.

Muir had previously written about Scottish literature as an up-and-coming critic in the early 1920s. Although he spent much time outside Scotland in these years, travelling in Europe and living in the south of England, his articles for the American *Freeman* included the fine essay 'A Note on the Scottish Ballads' and other Scottish essays such as that on George Douglas Brown ('George Douglas'). He contributed to the periodicals which MacDiarmid attempted to establish in the years after the First World War – one of the impulses behind MacDiarmid's efforts being the lack of a vital Scottish literary criticism and the lack of a Scottish literary periodical which could accommodate criticism of the quality of Muir's. Muir was also among the first critics to review favourably and with acute understanding MacDiarmid's early poems in Scots. Of the poem 'Country Life' from *Sangschaw*, he wrote: 'It is the product of a realistic, or more exactly a materialistic, imagination, which seizing upon everyday reality shows not the strange beauty which that sometimes takes on, but rather the beauty which it possesses normally and in use'.[3] He found *A Drunk Man Looks at the Thistle* 'the only poem of importance which has appeared in Scots since the death of Burns. . . . The flow, vigour, variety, wit, and originality of the poem are its greatest virtues'.[4]

Muir's Scottish prose writings have been ignored in most previous studies of his work, yet they provide firm evidence of his involvement with the history of Scottish culture and make clear the extent to which that history and culture have influenced him as poet. As we see in books such as *John Knox*, *Scottish Journey* and *Scott and Scotland*, and in the scripts of talks and programmes which he prepared for the Scottish BBC in the late 1930s and early 1940s when he was resident in St Andrews and Edinburgh, and again in the early 1950s during his Wardenship of Newbattle Abbey College, there were certain key periods and key figures in Scottish history for Muir, just as in the imagery of his poetry there were certain key figures in Greek myth to which he returned again and again. So far as Scottish history is concerned, he looked back to the period between Bannockburn and Flodden as a period with the potential for moral and cultural greatness in Scotland, where the inspiration of Wallace, the declaration of independence at Arbroath in 1320 and Barbour's apostrophe to freedom in *The Brus* were followed by the rich, distinctive Scots-language poetry of Dunbar, Henryson and Lyndsay, and where the Ballads gave voice to the life of the people. On the debit side were the personalities and climactic events which destroyed that potentiality: the tragic reign of Mary Stuart and the rise to power of Knox and Calvinism; the violent dissent and destructiveness of the Covenanters; the Unions of the Crowns and Parliaments; and the vacancy which he found at the heart of Scott's life and work, something which symbolised for him the vacancy at the heart of his country.

These key symbols are to be found in Muir's 1936 BBC programme for St Andrew's Day – a bleak recital which is a lament rather than a celebration of the national day. Muir's script details the desperate decline from the optimism of Barbour's freedom poem in an attempt to 'analyse the deep-set conflict of emotions, loyalties and beliefs, from which has emerged the Scotland of today'. Ironically, in this account it takes an Englishman, Cromwell, to restore temporary order to the disunited kingdom and to ask the warring religious dissenters to consider whether it is 'possible that you may be mistaken. There may be a covenant made with Death and Hell.'[5] In 'The Road to Fotheringay' (BBC 1943) and the later 'Heritage' programme 'The Inheritors' (1955), he sees Mary Queen of Scots as a fated figure who takes her place alongside the tragic characters of Greek myth:

> While on Linlithgow's lawns she at her play
> Holds her small court, already far away,
> Stretches the road that leads to Fotheringay . . .
>
> Now watch the puppets move into their place.[6]

Mary 'takes her way into the maze / From which no outlet is except the last';[7] 'she was in the net before she set a foot in Scotland'.[8]

Here, again, we have the obsession with determinism which activates so much of Muir's poetry; with the apprehension that the course of our life is already mapped out for us before we set out on it and that there would appear to be nothing that we ourselves can do to alter this. This is not how Muir believes human life should be lived, but how it appears to him that its nature frequently is, and nowhere does this seem to him to be so much in evidence as in the process of Scottish history. In both the 1943 and 1955 scripts, he sees Mary positioned at a turning point in that history.

> She was the first Scottish monarch to rule a Protestant nation; she was the last to represent the old kingdom. And standing there, she summed up in herself all the things, great and small, which were part of the old kingdom, and which were lost with it.[9]

Thus, for Muir, Scotland's loss of self-determination and identity was rooted in the tragedy of Mary and in the Calvinist Reformation of the mid-sixteenth century which destroyed the old traditions and left in their place a climate of dissension, intolerance and hostility to the creative imagination and its artistic achievements, a viewpoint which he developed more fully in *Scottish Journey*. He saw Scotland's impoverished cultural situation as having been exacerbated by the two Unions with England and by industrialisation, a process of increasing degradation for the ordinary working people of the country, and one which Calvinism encouraged by its emphasis on a work ethic which placed 'sanctioned greed' (*SJ* 103) before human welfare. In his memories of Glasgow, he contrasts the churchgoers with whom he associated when he first arrived in the city, who ignored the existence of the slums in the pursuit of personal social betterment, with the socialists and trades unionists who pledged themselves 'neither to take any advantage of their neighbours, nor to rise in the world at their expense' (*SJ* 147). He sees Calvinism, with its emphasis on the separation of the secular and the religious, its doctrine of the Elect and the consequent wish of its adherents to demonstrate through economic and social success that they are among the Chosen, as a religion which made it all too easy for the wretchedness of the poor to be ignored as a mark of God's disfavour and a hideous warning to others. In contrast, he himself saw the slum-dwellers' 'open publication of their degradation' as 'a last-ditch sentiment of justice. To publish one's degradation is a moral protest' (*SJ* 122).

In the artistic area, he contrasted the 'wedge of solid life' which the Ballads represented, the 'unchanging pattern of the Scottish spirit as it was before Protestant theology' (*SJ* 46), with the 'sham substitute' (*SJ* 67) provided by the Burns Cult and Kailyard literature. Just as he believed that Sir Walter Scott 'could swallow the most crude and worthless lumber if only it was sanctified by history' (*SJ* 58), so he finds the Burns Cult a 'myth . . . based on a firm foundation of sanctified illusion and romantic wish fulfilment. . . . The Burns of popular legend is an imaginative incarnation of a people's desires, unfulfilled in life. It has no fundamental resemblance to Burns himself' (*SJ* 90–1). On the other hand, what he calls 'the flight to the Kailyard' is to him understandable in the light of

> the rise of an industrial system so sordid and disfiguring that people were eager to escape from it by any road, however strange. The flight to the Kailyard was a flight to Scotland's past, to a country which had existed before Industrialism . . . To anyone living in Glasgow or Dundee even the Kailyard must have seemed heaven.

Nevertheless, 'by the time the flight took place Industrialism itself had sucked that tradition dry of its old vigour; it was no longer of importance except as a refuge from the hard facts of Scottish town life' (*SJ* 67–8).

Although *Scottish Journey* is on the surface the kind of travel book popular in the 1930s, Muir's journey from the Borders to the Orkneys is in reality an interior journey where description of landscape and social incident become a metaphor for a deeper psychological and philo-sophical search, what MacDiarmid in his similarly-conceived travel book *The Islands of Scotland* called the attempt 'to expose through the physical form the spiritual meaning of Scotland today'.[10] One finding which is especially relevant to Muir's assessment of Scottish history is the theme of betrayal, and his conclusion in *Scottish Journey* is that Scotland's decline is self-imposed through internal dissension:

> I went over in my mind what Scottish history I could remember, hoping to find some faint sign that Scotland's annals need not have been so calamitous as they were, and need not have led to the end of Scotland as a nation. I thought of the declaration of independence signed at Arbroath Abbey on April 6th, 1320: 'As long as a hundred of us remain alive, we will never submit to the domination of the English: for we fight not for glory, nor riches, nor honour, but for liberty alone, which no good man giveth up

save with life itself. I thought of Barbour's fine lines on freedom. But I reflected that Wallace had been betrayed, that David I had sold his country; I saw the first four Jameses thwarted on every side, Mary Stuart sold to the English, Charles I sold to the English, and Scotland itself sold to the English. I remembered Culloden and the Highland clans delivered helpless to Cumberland because of the intrigues and counter-intrigues of their chieftains and a few Lowland Scots ; I thought of the present feud between Glasgow and Edinburgh, the still continuing antipathy between the Highlands and the Lowlands; and it seemed to me that the final betrayal of Scotland which made it no longer a nation was merely the inevitable result, the logical last phase, of the intestine dissensions which had all through its history continued to rend it. (*SJ* 226–7)

In a striking image, he compares Scotland's fate to

a sight that I had seen as I stood on the banks of an Austrian mountain stream on a very hot summer day many years before. The stream was running very fast, and in the middle I made out two bright green snakes struggling in a death battle; I watched them for a few minutes; then they were both swept, still fighting, over a cataract. The comparison was too swift andd dramatic, I told myself, for the stubborn anger that burns through Scottish history; but nevertheless it would have been as impossible to put a stop to that at any of the disastrous turns of Scottish history. (*SJ* 227)

He concluded that

the real obstacle to the making of a nation out of Scotland lies now in the character of the people, which is a result of their history . . . And that obstacle, being the product of several centuries of life, is a serious one; it is, in fact, Scotland. (*SJ* 232)

Which one of us, having lived through Scotland's devious flirting with political self-responsibility in recent years, could disagree with his assessment?

A similarly pessimistic but more widely-disseminated assessment of Scotland's nationhood and culture took place in the book which followed *Scottish Journey*. After *An Autobiography*, *Scott and Scotland* is probably Muir's best-known Scottish prose book, and it has been a fruitful source of debate about the direction of Scottish literature and language since its publication in 1936. Over fifty years later, however, its bitter attack on the viability of Scotland's literature and language can be seen in its own historical perspective.

In *Belonging*, Willa Muir attributed the 'uncharacteristic acerbity' of *Scott and Scotland* to Muir's unhappy residence in St Andrews (*B* 195).

Yet the book was written at the beginning of that period, before the worst of their problems there manifested themselves, and its views on Calvinism and Scottish history and culture had been anticipated in *Scottish Journey* and in earlier periodical articles. In September 1931, for example, Muir had written of R. L. Stevenson in the *Bookman* that 'he had spent his childhood and youth in a country where everything combined to prevent an imaginative writer from coming to maturity',[11] while in a *Spectator* article, 'Literature in Scotland' in 1934, he had discussed the related problems of 'a renaissance without a centre' and the viability of the Scots language: 'that Scots will ever be used again as an independent language capable of fulfilling all the purposes of poetry and prose is, I should think, very doubtful'.[12]

There is a certain amount of truth in Muir's claims about the way in which the narrow, inflexible doctrines of the Reformed Church inhibited the healthy development of Scottish culture. His case in *Scott and Scotland*, however, is weakened by its extravagance and by its unwillingness to acknowledge the presence of other relevant factors. The often-quoted assertion that as a result of the retreat of the Scots language from formal functions and intellectual matters 'Scotsmen feel in one language and think in another' (*SS* 8), ignores a close relationship between Scots and English which made the adoption of 'sudroun' only too easy when it seemed socially and economically politic to do so. Similarly, he ignores the fact that any divided sensibility which developed in Scotland as a result of indigenous historical factors was almost certain to have been complicated by what was happening in England and Europe from the neoclassical movement of the seventeenth century onwards. Indeed, Muir's Cartesian separation of heart and head is strikingly similar to Eliot's theory of the dissociation of sensibility in 'the mind of England between the time of Donne or Lord Herbert of Cherbury and the time of Tennyson and Browning'.[13] He had previously been influenced by Eliot's critical theories in his 1921 essay 'A Plea for Psychology in Literary Criticism', and his *Variations on a Time Theme* of 1934 echoed Eliot's voice. It may well be that he was similarly influenced by Eliot when he began to examine the fragmentation of language and literature in Scotland.

Muir's analysis of the language situation is most unsatisfactory when he comes to consider the contemporary language and literature situation. He appears to take no account of the variety of language use in twentieth-century Scotland or of the fact that – even in the pre-television age of the 1930s and with radio in its infancy – for many Scots some Scottish form of English had become their *natural* language which they used, with appropriate register modifications, for both informal and formal purposes. His rigid distinction between Scots as the language of the heart at home and English as the language of formal affairs was no longer a meaningful distinction. Yet, as we see in *Scottish Journey*, he was in fact aware that Scottish English was now the language of a majority of Scots, and this silence in the text of *Scott and Scotland* does help to explain his lack of enthusiasm for MacDiarmid's Scots-language revival: 'Scots poetry can only be revived . . . when Scotsmen begin to think *naturally* in Scots' (*SS* 9). However, while hostility to an artificial assumption of Scots might be justified, there is no accompanying acknowledgement that there may still be poets, such as MacDiarmid himself, who will be able to develop a literary use of Scots from a strong base in the spoken Scots of their locality. Surprisingly, despite his earlier perceptive analyses of MacDiarmid's Scots lyrics and *A Drunk Man Looks at the Thistle*, he also seems unwilling to explore the potentiality of Scots as a literary medium which 'defamiliarises' in the manner discussed by formalist critics, by de Saussure in the field of linguistics and, in our own time, by post-structuralists such as Derrida with his concept of 'différance'. Formalist criticism was at work in the early decades of the century, a force that MacDiarmid himself was aware of; but in Muir's account of the Scots language situation, one again comes up against his lack of interest in formal analysis and the linguistic potentiality of a work of art, with a contrary concentration on its function in relation to social and moral/philosophical meaning. On the other hand, and to be fair to Muir, one has to acknowledge that, despite MacDiarmid's overt interest in the potentiality of language as language, as evidenced in his comments about the nature of Scots and in his practice in both Scots and later English-language poetry, he did throughout the 1920s and 1930s foreground the Scots language in a nationalist context as the only possible language for a revived Scottish nation and Scottish literature of consequence, while ignoring the fact that the equally nationalist-oriented fiction of a writer such as Neil M. Gunn was written in English and that he himself in the 1930s was increasingly turning to English in his poetry. In *Scott and Scotland*, therefore, Muir was attacking MacDiarmid on his chosen public ground, and an awareness of his own ambivalence in practice may have had no small influence on MacDiarmid's angry response to Muir's book.

While Muir's conclusion (paradoxically stated in his 'Introduction') that 'a Scottish writer who wishes to achieve some approximation to completeness has no choice except to absorb the English *tradition*' (*SS* 4; my italics) is equally unsatisfactory with his comments on language, there is considerable justification for his further charge that Scotland could not or would not support her artists. MacDiarmid himself had already given expression to such a problem in the confrontation between his Drunk Man and the Wheel of Life at the end of *A Drunk Man Looks at the Thistle*, in the themes of *To Circumjack Cencrastus* and in the events of his own life. Muir was at that time beginning to experience the problems of lack of recognition on his return from London to live in St Andrews, and his difficulties were to become more severe on the outbreak of war. Lack of support from their own country is a problem which many Scottish artists in literature, the visual arts and music have experienced and are still even at this late date in the century experiencing. It is, however, a different issue from the need to adopt the English tradition *in order to achieve completeness as a writer*. It may well be that to Muir, who had chosen to write in English as opposed to drawing on his Scottish roots and who was still in the mid-1930s trying to make a breakthrough in his poetry, MacDiarmid's astonishing poetry in Scots and his insistence that the way forward for a Scottish writer must be through Scots appeared as a threat to all he hoped to achieve. It was, perhaps, necessary for him to see MacDiarmid as something of an aberration: MacDiarmid 'has written some remarkable poetry; but he has left Scottish verse very much where it was before' (*SS* 9). What is clear is that neither, for whatever reason of his own, was able to acknowledge the variety of language use which was available at the time and which we now take for granted as one of the assets of the Scottish cultural situation today. Yet both Muir and MacDiarmid in their different ways contributed to that development of confident literary variety and flexibility.

Scott and Scotland caused a breach between Muir and MacDiarmid which was never healed, and this literary quarrel is yet another piece of evidence for the internal dissension which Muir saw as the reason for Scotland's decline. Once again, Scotland was the loser. Muir's articles on Scottish affairs became fewer in number and less provocative in the late 1930s and early 1940s, distanced in a way that the involved author of *Scottish Journey* and *Scott and Scotland* was not. Nor did he to any significant extent continue to comment on the revival in Scottish writing. His critical study *The Present Age*, which deals principally with English writers, gives a very brief mention to MacDiarmid, linking him with Roy Campbell (ironically the subject of MacDiarmid's vituperative satirical poem *The Battle Continues*) and finding that 'technically Campbell is by far the more accomplished poet'. Although, as in previous reviews, he commends *A Drunk Man* as the 'work of an interesting mind', he finds MacDiarmid's later poetry 'poor by comparison and often dull' (*PA* 115–16). While this view of the later poetry may in part be an accurate one, one can only regret Muir's withdrawal from a more active and extensive criticism of contemporary Scottish literature and of MacDiarmid in particular. As he himself commented in *Scott and Scotland*, the lack of a vital Scottish criticism meant that 'a really original Scots poet like Hugh MacDiarmid has never received in Scotland any criticism of his more ambitious poems which can be of the slightest use to him' (*SS* 22).

Despite the controversial nature of *Scott and Scotland*, Muir's writing in that book, as in his other Scottish-theme prose books and articles, makes his Scottish credentials clear. It is less easy to point to specifically Scottish characteristics when one comes to his poetry. Apart from a few ballad imitations in a light Scots among his early poems, Muir wrote in English, and obvious literary influences on his work came from English and German sources rather than from Scottish. While his boyhood island of Wyre was the inspiration behind the scenarios of his poems, the landscapes depicted in these poems are often symbolic landscapes, inhabited by mythical figures such as Penelope and Odysseus, Oedipus and the biblical Adam, and they therefore lack the specificity of locale which 'places' the work of other English-language Scottish writers such as Mackay Brown, Crichton Smith or Gunn.

Among the few poems which give overt expression to Muir's involvement with Scottish history are 'Scotland's Winter' and 'The Incarnate One' from *One Foot in Eden* and 'Scotland 1941' from *The Narrow Place*. The last two both demonstrate his hostility to Calvinism where 'the iron pen' has been substituted for the 'Word made flesh' and the work ethic has defeated spirituality and put in its place 'pride of pelf' (*CP* 213, 100). 'The Incarnate One', with its unforgettably Scottish opening:

> The windless northern surge, the sea-gull's scream,
> And Calvin's kirk crowning the barren brae
>
> (*CP* 213)

brings together the opposing worlds of Catholic Italy and Calvinist Scotland. The paintings of the Italian Giotto, in whose visual images one can experience 'the Word made flesh', are contrasted with the 'iron pen' of Scottish Calvinism through which 'the Word made flesh here is made word again . . . And God three angry letters in a book'. The Mystery has no place in the latter system; on its 'logical hook . . . the Mystery is impaled and bent / Into an ideological instrument', a negative transfiguration which is quietly underlined by the changing from upper- to lower-case letters (*CP* 213). As 'The Annunciation' from *One Foot in Eden* centres on the human love aspects of Incarnation, so here it is the impersonal inhumanity of Calvinism which is under attack. As with the essay 'Bolshevism and Calvinism', the poem then moves outwards from its religious censure into a confrontation with any ideological system which would enshrine the 'fleshless word'. Here, Muir once again emphasises that the self-sufficient impersonality of such systems can bring only 'abstract calamity' to human life (*CP* 214).

In addition to its attack on Calvinism, 'Scotland 1941' simultaneously takes up the theme of the Burns Cult, denouncing both Burns and Scott as 'sham bards of a sham nation' (*CP* 100). Yet, as we have seen from his prose writings, they are 'sham' not because of their own qualities but because the Scots have used them to forge a false historical image which has become a substitute for taking action to revitalise their unsatisfactory cultural present. While Scotland's agrarian, pre-Calvinist past may never have been so idyllic as the the the opening lines of 'Scotland 1941' suggest ('A simple sky roofed in that rustic day, / The busy cornfields and the haunted holms, / The green road winding up the ferny brae' (*CP* 100)), the idealisation, like Muir's view of the Kailyard, has its defence in the degradation which industrialisation meant for so many people. It is unfortunate that the poem was published in 1943 and entitled 'Scotland 1941', a period when Scotland, like Britain as a whole, was suffering in the war and could hardly be described as exhibiting 'spiritual defeat wrapped warm in riches'. For Scotland in 1941, 'our cities burning in their pit' meant the Clydebank blitz, not 'grinding dull lucre out'. Muir's portrait of contemporary Scotland as a museum-piece where 'Wallace and Bruce guard now a painted field' belongs more relevantly with MacDiarmid's satiric depictions of Scottish life in *A Drunk Man* and *To Circumjack Cencrastus* and with his own Scottish prose writings of the 1930s.

'Scotland's Winter' first appeared as epilogue to the chapter on Edinburgh in *Scottish Journey*, although it was not collected until *One Foot in Eden* twenty years later. Both it and 'Scotland 1941' were also used by Muir in his 1955 BBC script 'The Inheritors'. Unlike the satirical *Narrow Place* poem, 'Scotland's Winter' is a pure lament, where Scotland's decline is explored through the convention of the Scottish winter weather. The opening is heraldic in its icy metaphors:

> Now the ice lays its smooth claws on the sill,
> The sun looks from the hill
> Helmed in his winter casket,
> And sweeps his arctic sword across the sky.
>
> (*CP* 214)

The oblivious miller's daughter taps with her heels on the frozen ground under which Scotland's heroes lie. These heroes, unlike King Arthur's knights, cannot be awakened in Scotland's hour of need. Indeed, Muir seems to be suggesting that the 'common heels' of contemporary Scotland do not realise that they are in need of help. They

> do not know
> Whence they come or where they go
> And are content
> With their poor frozen life and shallow banishment.
>
> (*CP* 214)

The verse form underwrites the message of the poem. The irregularly-rhyming lines pattern the broken thread of nationhood as they gradually shrink from the five stresses of the opening line to the short, two-stress lines 'This land was kingless' and 'This land was songless' before opening out again into the sombre 'this land that with its dead and living waits the Judgment Day'. Within the idea of Judgment Day, there is the sense not only that the dead are waiting to be judged on their personal lives on earth, but also that dead and living will have to account for their inability to care for their country and its identity. The mood is one of sorrow and resignation as the gulf between Scotland's heroic past and impoverished present is contemplated.

'Scotland's Winter', like 'The Incarnate One' and 'Scotland 1941', is a strong, committed poem. Yet, as we have seen in the wider discussion of Muir's poetry, all three are unusual in their overt Scottish themes and references and in their involved perspective. It is in this context that *Scott and Scotland*'s extreme position with regard to language and tradition has worked to Muir's own disadvantage as a Scottish writer in addition to creating a false dichotomy in Scottish literature as a whole. Critics and readers have been only too willing to take Muir at his (apparent) self-estimation, and his poetry has on the whole been treated very much as if it belonged to English literature.

Yet despite its neutral English-language poetic surface and international and universal frames of reference, I would argue that Muir's poetry springs essentially from his response to his Scottish environment and culture, a culture in which religion has had a distinctive and dominant role, and where the specific doctrines of that religion seemed at variance with the values of the social community in which he grew up and with the aspiration towards self-knowledge and self-determination of the developing human being. This is not to say that the dominance of religion or the experience of a traditional, non-industrialised society are uniquely Scottish attributes. Clearly, they are not. Nevertheless, the particular form in which the religious spirit of Scotland has primarily been given expression since the Calvinist Reformation, and the interaction of that form of expression with forms of social ideology and organisation in the varied communities of rural and urban Scotland over the centuries, have produced a climate of ideas and attitudes which has informed the work of sufficient Scottish writers for one to recognise them as distinctively Scottish whatever their linguistic medium. Viewed in this context, Muir's themes deriving from the Fall of Man and the imagery in which they are expressed; his antithetical exploration of good and evil in human life; his search for a way of life which will give meaning to the individual life within a context of determinism; his insistence on cooperation and human solidarity and the essential relationship between the mundane and the spiritual can all be seen as taking their impulse from a Scottish ideology which in this century alone has produced writers as diverse as MacDiarmid, Carswell, Gunn, MacCaig, Crichton Smith, Spark, Jenkins and Gray, to name but a few. Apart from MacDiarmid's Scots and Crichton Smith's Gaelic poetry, the twentieth-century writers mentioned above use English as their linguistic medium. Yet no-one would question their intrinsic Scottish-ness, in addition to whatever non-local qualities they may have as writers. As Neil Gunn emphasised in many essays dealing with tradition and nationalism (which were, ironically, contemporaneous with *Scott and Scotland*), national identity arises from much more than language, although language is for most nations a primary element. The increasingly confident and distinctive writing in English which is currently emanating from the diverse cultures of the USA, Canada, Australia, the Caribbean and the continents of Africa and Asia underlines the limited nature of Muir's investigation of the place of language in Scottish literature. While this investigation may have played its part in keeping alive the debate about Scottish literary identity, it has, in my view, in the process distorted critical appreciation of his own work as a Scottish poet. This can be seen as being rooted in his response to Scottish history and culture and as embodying the qualities he himself found in Henryson: 'the fundamental seriousness, humanity and strength of the Scottish imagination' (*ELS* 21).

Muir's final contact with mainland Scotland was between 1950 and 1955 when he returned from Rome to take up a post as Warden of the newly reopened Adult Education College at Newbattle Abbey, near Edinburgh. Rome had been a time of fulfilment, but on his return to Edinburgh the seesaw took a downward swing and Muir found himself – as so often in his contacts with Scotland – entering into a period of tension and disagreement. On appointment to Newbattle, his dream had been of a residential institution which would give a fresh start to those who, like himself, had been excluded from post-school education. He had not been made aware, however, of Newbattle's insecure financial situation or of the small majority by which the decision to reopen the college had been taken. Inevitably, the difficult economic climate of the early 1950s brought increasing financial problems and with them pressure to run short-term and weekend courses which would bring in additional fees, a pragmatic change of policy which seems familiar in the 1990s but which ran counter to Muir's educational ideals. Worry and tension brought illness and the intimations of the heart trouble which was to affect him until his death. He resigned from Newbattle in 1955 when an invitation came to be Charles Eliot Norton Professor of Poetry at Harvard University for 1955–6. He wrote to Ernest Marwick of Orkney, who had been one of his mature students at Newbattle:

> I feel sad on leaving Newbattle, but the worries have been growing greater every year for the last four years, and finally I felt quite convinced that it would be unwise for me to try to cope with them any longer. Newbattle was a very pleasant place in the year that you were here, and I am so glad that you have pleasant memories of it. [14]

Muir says little about his Newbattle experience in his revised and extended autobiography, which was published in 1954 while he was still at the College. He concentrates on the generous gift of the Abbey by Lord Lothian 'to be used as a centre of liberal education, non-vocational and non-political', a vision which chimed with his own ideas about education; and on the intelligence and enthusiasm of the students who came into residence:

> I feel that, scattered in all sorts of odd jobs, in all parts of the country, there are countless men and women with an intellectual passion or an undeveloped gift, and that in most cases these remain lost or half-shaped, to their own misfortune and the general loss. (A 279–80)

Muir's students were fortunate. Among them were the writers George Mackay Brown, Tom Scott and Archie Hind. Some went on to university; a miner won a scholarship to Cambridge with a dissertation on Kant and a tube-maker with an essay on *Paradise Lost*. Several went to Ruskin College, Oxford.

As his ability to survive in so many unpromising situations might suggest, Muir was a much tougher character than he seemed to be from descriptions of his mild manner and general vagueness. In a broadcast after his death, H. Harvey Wood, who had appointed him to work for the British Council in Edinburgh in the later years of the war, described his ingenuity in organising programmes for the Allied Houses in Scotland, attracting to them 'in an unending stream, poets, musicians, critics, painters and sculptors, of all nationalities and of uniform distinction'. His business skills were apparently appreciated also, and he was 'a final court of appeal when, as so often, the monthly office accounts refused to balance'. Wood comments that 'he called forth the most affectionate and protective instincts of all my staff, and yet in many ways he was the most remote, the most self-sufficient of them all'.[15]

There are similar strong accounts of Muir from his other postings, and in Newbattle too he eventually routed, at least for a time, those who wished to destroy the liberal nature of the college as he envisaged it, before leaving to take up a visiting professorship at Harvard. Although on his return he settled not in Scotland but in the more climatically and intellectually sympathetic ambience of Cambridge, in the village of Swaffham Prior, his thoughts remained with Orkney. In December 1956, he wrote to Ernest and Janette Marwick about two ruined church towers which he could see from his cottage window: 'I am looking at the two towers as I write; as I cannot have the Castle in Wyre to look at they must serve me instead. I have become very fond of them'.[16] In October 1958, he wrote again: 'I would like to come up to Orkney next summer with Willa, if that is possible: I long to see it *once* more at least'.[17] His death in January 1959 prevented this, and he was buried not in Orkney but in Swaffham Prior churchyard.

NOTES

1. *The Spectator*, 6 October 1933, p. 434.
2. Edwin Muir, 'Christina Stead and Lewis Grassic Gibbon: *Seven Poor Men of Sydney*; *Grey Granite*', *The Listener* XII, 5 December 1934, p. 966. Reprinted in *The Truth of Imagination: Some Uncollected Reviews and Essays by Edwin Muir*, ed. P. H. Butter (Aberdeen: Aberdeen University Press, 1988), pp. 42–3.
3. Edwin Muir, 'The Scottish Renaissance', *Saturday Review of Literature*, 13 October 1925, p. 259.
4. Edwin Muir, Review of *A Drunk Man Looks at the Thistle, Nation and Athenaeum*, 22 January 1927, p. 568.
5. Edwin Muir, 'Saint Andrews Day', Scottish BBC, 30 November 1936. Script held in Glasgow University Theatre Archive, Special Collections Dept, STA ki Box 3/2.
6. Edwin Muir, 'The Road to Fotheringay', p. 1, Scottish BBC, 26 January 1945, Glasgow University Theatre Archive, Special Collections Dept, STA ki Box 3/2.
7. Ibid., script p. 4.

8. Edwin Muir, 'The Inheritors', Heritage Programme no 40, Scottish BBC, 27 March 1955, script p. 22, Glasgow University Theatre Archive, Special Collections Dept, STA ke Box 6.

9. Ibid., script p. 18.

10. Hugh MacDiarmid, *The Islands of Scotland* (London: Batsford, 1939), p. xix.

11. Edwin Muir, 'Robert Louis Stevenson', *Bookman* LXXIV, no 1, September 1931, p. 55.

12. Edwin Muir, 'Literature in Scotland', *The Spectator*, 25 May 1934, p. 823.

13. T. S. Eliot, 'The Metaphysical Poets', *Selected Essays*, 3rd enlarged ed. (London: Faber & Faber, 1951), p. 287.

14. Edwin Muir, Letter to Ernest Marwick, 19 August 1955, Orkney Archives D31/31/6.

15. H. Harvey Wood, 'Edwin Muir', Scottish BBC, 31 August 1969, script pp. 5–6, Glasgow University Theatre Archive, Special Collections Dept, STA Kc Box 7/6.

16. Edwin Muir, Letter to Ernest and Janette Marwick, 10 December 1956, Orkney Archives D31/31/6.

17. Edwin Muir, Letter to Ernest Marwick, 15 October 1958, Orkney Archives D31/31/6.

Six

A Difficult Country and our Home

One Foot in Eden and 'Last Poems'

Muir's Directorship of the British Institute in Rome from January 1949 until the summer of 1950 proved to be an especially fortunate period in his life. Daniel Hoffman has characterised the effect that Rome had on him as 'the northern child of Calvinism [being] awakened to a sensuous as well as a spiritual perception of what the Mediterranean world might take for granted'.[1] This perception had escaped Muir during his earlier stay in Italy in the 1920s when

> coming for the first time to the South, I was repelled by the violence of the colours, the sea like a solid lake of blue paint, the purple sky, the bright brown earth: to my unaccustomed eyes the contrasts seemed crude and without mystery. (*A* 210)

Now the Italian people, their landscape and the visible evidence of their history enchanted him. Rome offered 'the vistas at street corners where one looked across from one century to another' (*A* 277). He found in Italy as in Orkney 'the landscape, the soil . . . things shaped by generations with affection and made into a human scene' (*SL* 185). Especially influential was the religious atmosphere of Rome. He wrote to Joseph Chiari in December 1949:

> you feel the gods (including the last and greatest of them) have all been here, and are still present in a sense in the places where they once were. It has brought very palpably to my mind the theme of Incarnation . . . Edinburgh I love, but in Edinburgh you never come upon anything that brings the thought of Incarnation to your mind, and here you do so often, and quite unexpectedly. (*SL* 154)

One Foot in Eden reflects the influences of these contrary worlds of Catholic Rome and Protestant Scotland. The collection is divided into two sections. In Part I, themes predominantly of reconciliation are developed through the reworking of biblical and Greek myths, while in Part II the imagery belongs more to the world of everyday life and there is a partial return to a preoccupation with the kind of frustrations found in *The Labyrinth*. In its organisation, the collection thus exhibits overtly the dialectical method which had now become characteristic of Muir's poetry, a process akin to that of Blake's *Songs of Innocence and Experience* in which he presents us with the two 'contrary states of the human soul', most often in separate poems but sometimes within the confines of the one poem. As in Blake, both need to be seen as belonging together if a full understanding of the poetry is to be arrived at. In addition, while, like Blake and Shelley, he aspires towards a visionary ideal (and although Muir is closer to Blake in the religious nature of this ideal, he is perhaps closer to Shelley in relation to the elusiveness and ungraspability of the mystery), he is also like them committed to its application in the mundane world. He is no unworldly mystic seeking transcendence, but an active participant in the human drama.

By this stage in a reading of Muir's poetry, one is also becoming attuned to the unobtrusive but nevertheless identifiable poetic style which he had developed. There is his use of myth as a metaphor or code through which he can explore contemporary preoccupations. For Muir, 'a myth is endlessly adaptable' (*ELS* 58), and he is especially successful in his reworking of Greek myth, moulding it to his own purposes. There are also certain key legends and mythical figures which act as correlatives for his most recurring themes: Penelope faithful in the face of a fate she cannot know or influence; Oedipus treading his guilty way in innocence. This is similar to his practice in poems which have no recognisable mythic pattern, where one finds key words and phrases which have by regular use in a specific thematic context taken on their own symbolic function: words such as 'way', 'river', 'field', 'time', 'harvest'. Symbolism is increasingly present in the late poetry, and *The Narrow Place* in particular demonstrates how Muir often infuses very ordinary domestic words such as 'hearthstone', 'family', 'walls' and 'harvest' with symbolic implications so that the traditional, positive qualities inherent in them are used to highlight the negative, destructive nature of the situation being described or enacted. In addition, although his work does not have the surface linguistic excitement of an Eliot or MacDiarmid, in his late poetry he is able to manipulate syntax and blank verse rhythms to produce, as did Wordsworth, a flexible narrative or reflective poetic medium. He follows Hölderlin in his condensed communication of a paradoxical or not readily reconcilable concept through his linking of the opposing elements by the unifying conjunction 'and', and in his positive employment of ambivalence and ambiguity. In many poems, he makes effective use of a short, simple, ballad-like stanza in conjunction with

complexity of philosophical content, while his handling of the sonnet
form or a modified version of it is always assured. All of these stylistic
features can be seen in operation in *One Foot in Eden*, together with new
developments in metonymic and allegoric modes.

Part I of the collection is divided between biblical and Greek myth
poems on a ratio of 2:1 – a surprising finding because the strength of the
poems deriving from Greek legend is such that one has the impression
that their number is greater than it actually is. This may be because the
myths chosen are essentially related to the philosophical questions
which most preoccupied Muir as man and poet. In addition, the fact
that these myths were for him 'stories' and as such not related to personal
religious belief may have enabled him more confidently to reshape
them.

Some of these Greek myth poems focus on the human and
reconciliatory features of a given experience. Others, like 'The Other
Oedipus', are equivocal in their communication and appear to deal more
with the evasion of personal responsibility. In this poem, the pain of
human experience is evaded through madness, a theme similar to that
explored in earlier poems such as 'Hölderlin's Journey' and 'Troy'.
Oedipus is portrayed as a broken, mad old man who, like Lear and his
fool, travels the road with serving-boy and concubine. Lear's madness,
however, was a temporary escape from a reality too overwhelming to be
borne, and out of it came eventually greater understanding. There are
no such positive implications here. Oedipus and his companions
are happy to remain in their state of madness. 'Gay and innocent', for
them 'fate [has been] sent on holiday'. However the price in Muir's
terms is high. Like the unmemoried animals in the poem 'The
Animals', 'they were quite storyless and had clean forgotten / That
memory burning in another world'. Their life is a negation of the
'articulate breath' of human existence. Thus, 'the surly Spartan farmers /
Were kind to them, pitying their happiness' (*CP* 201).

Two of the most powerful of these Greek myth poems are 'Orpheus'
Dream' and 'Telemachos Remembers', both of which stress the power of
love in the face of adversity. In the popular version of the Orpheus and
Eurydice myth, Orpheus loses Eurydice permanently to the underworld
because his love for her forces him to break his agreement with Pluto
that he will not look back until he is out of Hades. In the account in
Plato's *Symposium*, the gods show Orpheus only the ghost or shadow of
Eurydice, thus leaving him to return to earth without her real self.
Muir's poem is a reversal of both these stories, but is particularly related
to Plato's 'shadow' version in that the love between Orpheus and
Eurydice is so great that it in the end overcomes their separation. It is

Pluto who must be content to keep the shade, the 'poor ghost of Eurydice . . . Alone in Hades' empty hall', while the reunited lovers 'dare / At last to turn our heads and see' that underworld shadow figure (*CP* 201).

Like many of Muir's best poems, 'Orpheus' Dream' is ambivalent in meaning in that, as Muir said of Hölderlin, 'the mystery itself, not any particular manifestation of it, was his theme' (*ELS* 103). The title immediately brings us up against the dreamworld/reality opposition. Yet dream in Muir's poetry, as in his life, is very often a way of coming into contact with significant truths; it is not an evasion of reality as in the conventional interpretation of 'daydream' or as in the madness of Oedipus or the old man in the Troy sewers. The ultimate message of the poem – the triumph of love – is clear, but Muir leaves the details imprecise, and in this he is helped by the confusion generated by the dream context:

> And she was there. The little boat
> Coasting the perilous isles of sleep,
> Zones of oblivion and despair,
> Stopped, for Eurydice was there.
> The foundering skiff could scarcely keep
> All that felicity afloat . . .
>
> (*CP* 200)

What are these 'perilous isles of sleep', and where exactly is the little boat journeying? In the waters of Lethe, underworld river of forgetfulness, or in Orpheus's imagination, or both? Who is in the boat with him? Eurydice herself or his vision of her? Who are the 'we' of the final stanza? Has he recaptured the real Eurydice, or is their union one of the spirit only? Here, the relationship with Plato's version is significant, because there is a link with Platonic philosophy in Muir's implication that the reality of the lovers' relationship lies not in their material circumstances but in what lies beyond these.

From a formal point of view, the poem demonstrates once again Muir's unobtrusive technical maturity in these late poems. The immediacy of the opening statement, 'And she was there', catches and holds the experience which is then substantiated in the development of the poem. The pause after the first word 'Stopped' in the fourth line of the first stanza and the balancing of polysyllabic words such as 'afloat', 'foundering' and 'felicity' with the short 'skiff' and 'keep', together with the repeated 'f', 's' and 'k' sounds which move forwards and backwards across the lines, bring to life the rocking movement of the boat, almost overturned by the emotion of its occupants. Throughout the poem, the placing of significant words such as 'won', 'whole', 'good' and 'dare' in a strong position at the end of a rhythmically rising line reinforces the positive nature of the lovers' experience, as does the circular, unifying *abccba* rhyming pattern of the stanzas. As with the 'she' of the first stanza, the 'we' of the second stanza is ambivalent: 'As if we had left earth's frontier wood / Long since . . .'. The most obvious reading relates to Orpheus and his newly-found Eurydice, but there is a sense in which the reader and all humanity are also drawn into the experience by this inclusive pronoun – a widening of the original context supported by the phrase 'from this sea had won / The lost original of the soul', with its implications of Eden and the Fall. The final stanza provides a lasting transfiguration experience which is a reversal of the original myth. The lovers can now together dare to look back to the underworld. Love has conquered death, however the ambivalent individual details of the poem's scenario may be interpreted.

The power of love is also the message of 'Telemachos Remembers'. This late version of the Penelope/Odysseus story, which had long fascinated Muir, brings together the opposing forces of faith and uncertainty so that a possible way forward is opened up. The poem gains much from being narrated by Telemachos, who, from his dual standpoint of child and adult, is able to communicate both the apparent chaos and futility of his mother's task as he saw it when a child, and his mature adult's understanding of its underlying significance. As in a previous adaptation of the legend such as 'The Return of Odysseus' from *The Narrow Place*, one is aware here of the theme of a predestined way of which humans are necessarily ignorant. Yet the emphasis in the poem is not on this restricted way but on the potential within the human situation and on Penelope's personal decision to *choose* the direction of her life in keeping faith with Odysseus, even though she cannot be sure of his return and even if the decision means that she, as a result, gives up the possibility of personal achievement in her own life.

In a BBC broadcast in 1954, Muir himself drew attention to a life/art opposition in the poem, an interpretation which is relevant also to his further development of the theme in 'Song for a Hypothetical Age'. Had Penelope finished her weaving, she would in Muir's words 'have achieved the supreme work of art, but in doing so would have renounced her humanity'.[2] The emphasis is therefore placed firmly on the importance of the human dimension and on the power of human love.

In the bleaker 'Song for a Hypothetical Age' from Part II, however, the theme is as in *The Narrow Place* contextualised negatively. Penelope is still given as the exemplar of faith and humanity, but the section of the poem which refers to her is placed in parenthesis and the speaker looks back to her from 'our new impersonal age'. As Mansie Manson found in *Poor Tom*, grief has no place in the Marxist dream, but loss of the capacity to grieve means also the loss of one's humanity. Penelope's story has no relevance 'where everything is in its place / And happiness inevitable'. Yet, where grief has been exiled, joy too 'no more shall wake' (*CP* 223–4). These reconciliation poems of *One Foot in Eden* do not come easily, and Muir never forgets the contrary negative scenario.

Reconciliation themes are prominent in the biblical myth poems of the collection. In *An Essay on Criticism*, Graham Hough has commented on the difficulty posed by the attempt to use the Christian myth for literary purposes. While 'in very early mythologies alternative creation myths, alternative genealogies of the gods make their appearance' without any apparent conflict between them, it is not so with the Christian myth. In Hough's view, 'those who maintain that the Christian myth is different from all others are right – not because it is "truer" than any other, but because it was believed in a different way'.[3] In this regard, I believe that the most successful of Muir's biblical or Christian myth poems are those in which he uses the myth in a free way, adapting it to his own needs as he does the Greek myths.

One of the finest of these poems is 'The Annunciation'. In the letter from Rome to his friend Joseph Chiari quoted at the beginning of this chapter, Muir speaks of the ever-present sense of Incarnation in the Rome atmosphere, and goes on to express his hope that he will be able to 'write a few poems about that high and difficult theme sometime'. He found himself, however, 'rather afraid of writing on such a theme and though it occupies my mind whenever my mind is free from daily affairs, I feel nothing is ready yet to be written down' (*SL* 154–5). 'The Annunciation' took its starting point from the experience of

> stopping for a long time one day to look at a little plaque on the wall of a house in the Via degli Artisti, representing the Annunciation. An angel and a young girl, their bodies inclined towards each other, their knees bent as if they were overcome by love, 'tutto tremante', gazed upon each other like Dante's pair; and that representation of a human love so intense that it could not reach further seemed the perfect earthly symbol of the love that passes understanding. (*A* 278)

It thus concentrates not on the traditional transcendental aspects of the meeting between angel and girl, but once again on the human dimension of an experience. Yet this is done in a way that does not cancel out the mystery of the happening. Such an experience could never have come to the 'congregations of the north' to whom this 'open

declaration' which to Muir seemed 'the very mark of Christianity' would
have appeared to be a 'sort of blasphemy, perhaps even an indecency'
(*A* 278). In 'The Annunciation', it provoked an eroticism rare in Muir's
poetry:

> Immediacy
> Of strangest strangeness is the bliss
> That from their limbs all movement takes.
> Yet the increasing rapture brings
> So great a wonder that it makes
> Each feather tremble on his wings.
>
> (*CP* 206)

The religious myth poems which came out of the Rome experience
are notable for their focusing on the humanity that he found there. As
'The Annunciation' centres on human as opposed to transcendental love,
so the emphasis in 'Adam's Dream' is not on the loss of Eden but on
Adam's acceptance of his new life in time as father of his human
children. It is a strong poem thematically and stylistically. The reader is
immediately pulled into the drama through Muir's manipulation of a
visual perspective which extends from Adam 'high on the mountain-
side, bare crag behind' to the plane reaching into the distance in front of
him where 'a few small figures [were] running / That were like men and
women, yet were so far away / He could not see their faces' (*CP* 196).
Adam's confusion is compounded by the continuous though constantly
interrupted running movement of the figures, a movement communicated to the reader through short, punctuated phrases of contrasting
terms:

> On they ran,
> And fell, and rose again, and ran, and fell,
> And rising were the same yet not the same,
> Identical or interchangeable,
> Different in indifference.
>
> (*CP* 196)

In places, the poem returns to the kind of experience depicted in 'The
Labyrinth' in its communication of Adam's bewilderment at this 'way
that was not like a way'. His shouted questioning and the crags'
*un*answering echoing of the questions bring back the claustrophobic
unresponsiveness of 'The Way' with its relentless burden of 'the way
leads on' (*CP* 159).

Gradually, the focus of the poem is shortened from the long range of
the opening images until Adam is placed *among* the running figures.

This shifting focus is paralleled in the time shift from Adam dreaming in his present to a future that is beyond him but which is our present; to his eventual remembrance and acceptance of his past which has become the context of our spiritual journey. There is a philosophical change too from his position as a son of God, set apart from man although fallen, to the involved father of his human children who 'took their hands / That were his hands, his and his children's hands'. The poem thus ends with the emphasis on human love, a position reinforced by its closing lines with their reconciling conjunction 'and': Adam 'cried out and was at peace, and turned again / In love and grief in Eve's encircling arms' (*CP* 197).

In 'The Days', it is the Genesis creation myth which is reworked, and once again Muir adapts the biblical story freely and in a way which leaves the focus on the human story. In this poem, his earlier practice of using certain key words and phrases as recurring symbols is extended into the area of metonymy and synecdoche. Thus the eerie desolation of a planet without vegetation or animal or human life and the 'inhuman burgeoning' of the first 'hard and rocky spring' is communicated through synecdochic imagery:

> And nothing there for claw or hand,
> Vast loneliness ere loneliness began,
> Where the blank seasons in their journeying
> Saw water at play with water and sand with sand.
> (*CP* 194)

The creation of the animals is represented by their traditional king, the lion, 'raging and burning in its watery cave' and by Muir's personal symbol of awe-inspiring animal life, the horse. Then comes man, and the change which he brings is symbolised as in the poem 'The Animals' by the fact of language, 'the articulate breath'. The unity of all creation is depicted by the recurring key symbol of the river, flowing from its source in the mountains, 'threading, clear cord of water, all to all'; and syntactically in one long sentence, which runs from this point to the end of the poem, in which the nature of human life is again depicted in metonymic and emblematic terms. Although symbols standing in for a fuller action, these items are in no way abstract in nature but are derived from common features of everyday life. They include 'the wooded hill and the cattle in the meadow'; 'the tall wave breaking on the high sea-wall'. There is the fine visual symbol of 'the crescent shadow / Of the light-built bridge', symbolising both communication and man's technical achievement. Food-gathering finds the 'fish in the billow's heart, the man with the net'; war 'the hungry swords crossed in the cross of warning'; Scotland's heroic past 'the lion set / High on the banner, leaping into the sky'. The poem ends with the vision of the reconciliation and transfiguration which God's Sabbath will ultimately bring, its vision patterned in the interconnected syntax and the gradually lengthening lines which lead us into the final 'seventh great day and the clear eternal weather' (*CP* 195).

One of Muir's best-known poems is 'One Foot in Eden', and it is this poem which most conspicuously brings together his antithetical view of human existence, the reconciliation between its opposing elements and the firm focus on the positives of human life which become increasingly dominant in his later work. As we have seen, his experience of Catholic Rome played a large part in his attainment of a psychological and spiritual equilibrium. Yet, however unfortunate many of his experiences in Scotland had been and were again to be during his term at Newbattle, the influence of Scottish culture and religion ran deeply within him, and it does not seem fanciful to see these polar experiences as lying behind the reconciliation theme of poems such as 'One Foot in Eden' and its plainer – perhaps more Scottish – version, 'The Difficult Land' of Part II of the collection.

In 'One Foot in Eden', the metaphor of reconciliation is an agricultural one. Here, the biblical parable of the tares and wheat is reversed as the speaker recognises that 'nothing now can separate / The corn and tares compactly grown'. The emblematic nature of the imagery of harvest – 'The armorial weed in stillness bound / About the stalk' – creates an atmosphere of timelessness while the shifting pronouns effect a change in perspective from the observing 'I' of the first two lines of the first verse to the subsequent inclusive 'we' and 'our' as the speaker involves himself with the 'outside Eden' life. Muir's insight here is that whatever time and life have made of what we *could* have been, 'yet still from Eden springs the root / As clear as on the starting day'. The original innocence is still within us; and not only is this essence still in our lives, but human life itself brings forth its own particular virtues, born out of difficulty and suffering, which are equally worthy of acceptance as the unfallen state that he had previously mourned:

> But famished field and blackened tree
> Bear flowers in Eden never known.
> Blossoms of grief and charity
> Bloom in these darkened fields alone.
> What had Eden ever to say
> Of hope and faith and pity and love
> Until was buried all its day

> And memory found its treasure trove?
> Strange blessings never in Paradise
> Fall from these beclouded skies.
>
> (*CP* 212–13)

The poet's aim is no longer to retrace the human journey 'in imagination's one long day' (*CP* 66) but to sing the blessings of the here and now, however painfully achieved.

That such reconciliation is not easily achieved can be seen in poems such as 'The Cloud' and 'The Difficult Land' from Part II of the collection, which, like 'Song for a Hypothetical Age', return us to a position where the negative view of human life appears dominant. 'The Cloud' seems to draw on the dark experiences of Prague. Driving to the Writers' House in Bohemia, its speaker and his companion 'lost our way / In a maze of little winding roads that led / To nothing but themselves' (*CP* 225). Suddenly they come upon 'a young man harrowing, hidden in dust . . . A pillar of dust moving in dust'. Unlike Wordsworth's 'solitary Highland Lass' whose song links past, present and future, singer and listener, and passes into the poet's inmost being to provide sustenance and renewal, Muir's solitary harrower 'seemed / A prisoner walking in a moving cloud / Made by himself for his own purposes'. What was for Wordsworth a moment of insight is for Muir a symbol of despair: a barren, cheerless encounter which points to aridity and imprisonment in human life. The message of the encounter is reinforced by the perverse message of the speaker at the Writers' House who 'praised the good dust, man's ultimate salvation, / And cried that God was dead'. In the face of such emptiness, the poet can only hope for something akin to God's grace which will show him that the impersonal calamity enacted in so many poems of *The Labyrinth* collection and here again in 'The Cloud' is not irremediable and that the apparently 'blindfold mask on a pillar of dust' is in fact the 'face once broken in Eden / Beloved, world-without-end lamented face' (*CP* 226).

The ambience of 'The Difficult Land' appears at first sight to relate to that of 'The Cloud'. We are once again in a situation of restriction and arbitrary happening: 'Here things miscarry / Whether we care, or do not care enough. . . . We yoke the oxen, go out harrowing, / Walk in the middle of an ochre cloud' (*CP* 219). The difference is that the people in 'The Difficult Land' are not isolated, turned in on themselves. Despite the frustrations of an existence where 'sun, rain and frost alike conspire against us', they are bound together by their sense of community and ancestral ties, aspects of living which, as we have seen, Muir stressed increasingly in late prose work such as 'The Poetic Imagination' and *The*

Estate of Poetry. Through the employment of recognisable key words, the speaker of 'The Difficult Land' gives expression to Muir's positives, attributes which the protagonists of poems such as 'The Usurpers', 'The Ring' and 'The Cloud' have lost or have denied:

> We are a people; race and speech support us,
> Ancestral rite and custom, roof and tree,
> Our songs that tell of our triumphs and disasters
> (Fleeting alike), continuance of fold and hearth,
> Our names and callings, work and rest and sleep,
> And something that, defeated, still endures –
> These things sustain us.
>
> > (*CP* 219–20)

The positives put forward here are the attributes of his upbringing in the cooperative society of Orkney, qualities stressed also by the novelist Neil M. Gunn in his many books and essays on the Highland way of life: the importance of 'growing and blossoming from our own roots',[4] of not leaving the past and its happenings 'nameless',[5] of cooperation as opposed to competition. So Muir's speakers are

> drawn back again
> By faces of goodness, faithful masks of sorrow,
> Honesty, kindness, courage, fidelity,
> The love that lasts a life's time. And the fields,
> Homestead and stall and barn, springtime and autumn.
> (For we can love even the wandering seasons
> In their inhuman circuit.) And the dead
> Who lodge in us so strangely, unremembered,
> Yet in their place.
>
> > (*CP* 220)

Thus, despite its dispiriting opening, this poem is a companion piece to 'One Foot in Eden'. It perhaps draws more on Muir's Scottish environment than does that poem, which seems to have taken its impulse from the warmth and humanity which he found so attractive in Rome. Both nevertheless demonstrate an acceptance and a celebration of this 'other land' which, although a 'difficult country', is 'our home' (*CP* 212, 220).

Two companion poems which seem to speak of a preoccupation with old age and approaching death are 'The Late Wasp' and 'The Late Swallow', allegorical poems which remind one also of Muir's admiration for the poetry of the fifteenth-century Scottish makar Robert Henryson. As we have seen, Muir was interested in Henryson's use of allegory, 'which finds in the lives of the animals a pattern of human life. It has obvious merits; it simplifies life; it so reduces the dimensions of the human situation that we can easily grasp them.' He makes special mention in his essay on Henryson of 'The Preiching of the Swallow', a fable in which he finds that 'Henryson achieves a profound effect of tragedy and pity. . . . The poem produces a strong feeling of approaching danger and of a blindness that no warning can pierce' (*ELS* 14, 16).

Muir's comments on Henryson's *Fables* can be applied to his own allegories of Wasp and Swallow. Despite its easy, companionable opening tone and rhythmic movement, 'The Late Wasp' is ultimately the bleaker of the two. Its tightly-constructed fourteen lines move from the intimate opening to its concluding bleakness and echoing of Yeats, where 'the good air will not hold' and there is nothing left for this late summer visitor but to 'dive through nothing and through despair'. Behind the allegorical figure of the wasp is a pessimistic view of the human journey, simplified and, as Muir said of Henryson's allegories, reduced to dimensions that we can easily grasp. Time, the enemy he had long feared, has eventually caught up with the poet. For him, too, 'the familiar avenues of the air / Crumble now, crumble' (*CP* 233).

'The Late Swallow' presents an antithetical view of the situation. It captures the concern of Henryson's admonitory swallow in its short, urgent opening lines, but here it is the bird which is the endangered one, as opposed to its being the prophet of approaching danger. As with the wasp's situation, winter is coming and already its companions 'all have flown / To seek their southern paradise . . . And you are alone' (*CP* 233). Behind the exhortation to the bird, one senses once again the ageing poet's exhortation to himself. For him, too, the movement should be 'across the great earth's downward sloping side'. 'Why should you cling / Still to the swiftly ageing narrowing day?' The poem's sixteen lines modulate from the urgency of its opening to a positive vision of the ultimate ending of the human journey in its closing lines. The exhortation to leave is not after all a warning to avoid approaching danger, but a recognition of the need to prepare for the final journey: 'Till falling down the homing air / You light and perch upon the radiant tree' (*CP* 233). The allegorical method employed here allows the poet to state his belief in immortality in an open way, while, taken together, the poems enact the contrasting yet complementary responses to the mystery of human existence which Muir had explored since his earliest poetry.

Finally, there is 'The Horses', one of the most anthologised of Muir's poems, but one which reflects its author's increasing concern with the

threat of nuclear war in the 1950s, the period of the 'Cold War' between
the superpowers. Although not overtly divided into sections, the poem
does have two distinct movements: an opening movement where the
details of the devastation and the surviving community's response to the
disaster are outlined, and a visionary second part where the hope for a
new beginning is symbolised in the coming of the strange horses and
the relationship that they offer to the surviving humans.

The opening lines offer a corollary to the creation process depicted in
Genesis and in the poem 'The Days'. As God created the world in six
days and rested on the seventh, so man, his final creation, has taken a
similar period to destroy it and reduce it to silence. As in 'The Days',
Muir adopts a metonymic approach to the detailing of the disaster. The
dependence on mechanisation and technology which he deplored in the
essay 'The Poetic Imagination' and the resulting 'abstract calamity'
brought about about by the adherence to ideologies which deny values
of tradition and cooperation and concern for the individual are
represented by the failed, dumb radios; the tractors in the fields, useless
without their fuel and spare parts; the plane plunging into the sea; the
warship with its 'dead bodies piled on the deck'. According to the
speaker of the poem, the survivors are content to leave aside such
evidence of the failure of our modern world. In anticipation of George
Mackay Brown's similar message in the short story 'The Wireless Set',[6]
Muir's radios are silent and will be left that way:

> But now if they should speak,
> If on a sudden they should speak again,
> If on the stroke of noon a voice should speak,
> We would not listen, we would not let it bring
> That old bad world that swallowed its children quick
> At one great gulp. We would not have it again.

They are content also to let the tractors lie and rust 'like dank sea-
monsters couched and waiting. . . . We make our oxen drag our rusty
ploughs, / Long laid aside' (*CP* 227).

As we have already seen in the splendid description of his father's
horses in *An Autobiography* and in an earlier version in *The Three Brothers*,
the horse inspired in Muir feelings of fascination and awe. He now
recreates this sense by the suspenseful manner in which he brings the
horses into the poem and by the kind of imagery used to depict them.
As with many of the late poems, 'The Horses' is written in a flexible
blank-verse form which enables him to move freely, pausing and
restarting where he will, putting the emphasis where it needs to go.
Thus, 'Late in the summer the strange horses came', with its stress on

the opening 'Late' and subsequent stresses on 'summer', 'strange horses' and 'came', together with the pause in the movement after 'came', prepares us for listening. Just as in 'Adam's Dream' Muir created a sense of visual perspective, so now he creates an aural perspective. First there is a 'distant tapping', then a 'deepening drumming' – the closer sound marked by the alliteration and the change from the softer 't' and 'p' to the stronger 'd', 'dr' and 'mm' of 'drumming'. The sound 'stopped, went on again / And at the corner changed to hollow thunder'. There is a long pause in the short line 'We saw the heads' which leaves one in suspense until it is completed by the surge of the following line with its 'Like a wild wave charging and were afraid'. As the mechanical tractors had been compared to 'dank sea-monsters couched and waiting', menacing, yet inert, so this sea metaphor of the 'wild wave' seems to symbolise the energy and cleansing natural power of the horses. The awe of the watchers and the extraordinary nature of the horses is captured in their depiction as 'fabulous steeds set on an ancient shield'. The young colts bring with them the innocence of the unfallen world. It is not clear where they have come from: it is 'as if they had been sent / By an old command to find our whereabouts'. The grace offered through them and their offer of 'free servitude' and 'long-lost archaic companionship' changes the lives of the survivors: 'their coming our beginning' (*CP* 227).

'The Horses' is a powerful and moving poem, and this is in large measure due to the imaginative strength of its visionary section. It is, however, only a partial statement of Muir's response to the threat of nuclear war. For a contrary but complementary working-out of the situation posited, one has to turn to 'After a Hypothetical War' from his posthumously-published 'Last Poems'.

After Muir's death, Willa Muir and J. C. Hall put together a group of poems under the title of 'Poems not previously collected' and included this as the final section in the *Collected Poems* of 1960. Three groups of poems were included: twenty-two poems either published during Muir's lifetime or given by him to his publishers in typescript form; six typescript poems discovered among his papers and previously unpublished; and a group of poems in manuscript form. These poems have now been included as 'Last Poems' in the 1991 edition of *Complete Poems*.

As a result of their posthumous collection, the poems inevitably vary in quality and state of finish. What is striking about them, however, is the continuation to the very end of Muir's working life of his open-ended investigation of the human situation and his involvement with the happenings of the late 1950s. Some of the poems were motivated by his stay in America between 1955 and 1956. Many are preoccupied with the threat of nuclear war explored in 'The Horses'. Unlike the regenerative outcome envisaged in that poem, however, the message of the posthumous poems is that of Henryson's prophetic bird in 'The Preiching of the Swallow': 'This grit perrell I tauld thame mair than thryis; / Now ar thay deid, and wo is me thairfor'.[7]

'After a Hypothetical War', with its vision of the 'purblind peasant squatting, elbows out / To nudge his neighbour from his inch of ground', the 'chaotic breed of misbegotten things, / Embryos of what could never wish to be' and men who are 'dumb and twisted as the envious scrub' (*CP* 243), thus presents an opposing scenario to that of 'The Horses'. Read together, they dramatise more comprehensively the moral choices facing human beings and the outcomes present within them. Despite our contemporary dismantling of Cold War machinery, the acuity and prophetic nature of Muir's response to the nuclear threat has been validated in the years since he wrote by scientific awareness of the possibility of 'nuclear winter', of the fact there could be no 'nuclear theatres' with the corollary of safe havens somewhere on the planet which even the most pessimistic of science-fiction writers tended to envisage; we are all bound together in the face of such potential ultimate disaster. The poem is one of the earliest artistic statements of the horrors that nuclear war would bring, and it was written at a time when official propaganda, very often backed up by scientific statement, put forward the view that such a war could be contained; that there would be survivors who could continue with the life they had known. The contemporary horror of the Gulf War and the dereliction it has caused for so many of the peoples of Iraq, the descent into chaos of the former Yugoslavia and the re-emergence of fascist ideology in various parts of Europe fuel fears of further conflicts and make Muir's poem of continuing relevance despite the changed nuclear context.

Poems such as 'The Last War', 'The Day before the Last Day' and 'The Refugees Born for a Land Unknown' continue his preoccupation with war and its aftermath. The first mentioned, like 'After a Hypothetical War', is one of the poems which carry Muir's imprimatur; the second and third belong to the group of manuscript poems. 'Shall we all die together?', the speaker of 'The Last War' asks, and proceeds to explore the horror of this final war in which there is 'no place at all for bravery . . . No way to attempt, to save / By our own death the young that they might die / Sometime a different death' (*CP* 257, 256). The death of nature and human life is pictured metonymically as we watch 'bird and tree / Silently falling . . . And we see our bodies buried in falling birds'. As we realise that the 'articulate breath' has become 'the lexicon of a dream', dead as the dictionary of dead languages, the greatest pain is perhaps the knowledge that we are ourselves responsible for the disaster. This insight is communicated initially in striking *imagiste* terms – 'A tree thin sick and pale by a north wall, / A smile splintering a face' – and followed by an acknowledgement of our rejection of communal belonging and responsibility:

> Because we could not wait
> To untwist the twisted smile and make it straight
> Or render restitution to the tree.
>
> (*CP* 257–8)

Muir's alternative positive scenario in this grouping of posthumous poems is presented in poems which, like the letters to the Marwicks from Swaffham Prior and the notes which he kept of his dreams at this period, show him returning at the end of his life to thoughts of home, family and childhood: poems such as 'The Brothers', 'There's nothing here' and 'I have been taught'. 'The Brothers' took its impulse from a dream which he had about his own brothers in which he saw them not in the competitive attitudes of youth, but transfigured. He wrote to Kathleen Raine that they appeared to him 'infinitely happy in making each other happy, and all that was left in their hearts and their bodies was grace' (*SL* 191). 'I have been taught' is one of the group of manuscript poems and the last poem printed in *Collected Poems*. Although obviously unrevised, it is a fitting tribute to the impulses behind his poetry and to its searching nature:

> I have been taught by dreams and fantasies
> Learned from the friendly and the darker phantoms
> And got great knowledge and courtesy from the dead
> Kinsmen and kinswomen, ancestors and friends
> But from two mainly
> Who gave me birth . . .
>
> And now that time grows shorter, I perceive
> That Plato's is the truest poetry,
> And that these shadows
> Are cast by the true.
>
> (*CP* 274)

The poems in *One Foot in Eden* and 'Last Poems' foreground in a particularly compelling way the antithetical nature of Muir's poetry. It is not the artist's function to present us with solutions to the problems which face us, but through the enactment of the possibilities within a given situation to make us aware of our motivations and choices, of the implications of our actions and of the nature of the circumstances in which we have to operate. One of the most significant aspects of Muir's poetry, in my view, is the way in which he opens up the choices before us and makes us more fully aware of the nature of human life: what it is and what it could be, in both positive and negative terms. In the developed world at least, twentieth-century human beings have rejected the communal, cooperative way of living which writers such as Muir and Gunn looked to as a healthy order of society. Yet Muir's poems of the Second World War and Cold War periods point to the inescapable fact that while we may have rejected communal belonging in our social organisation, we cannot escape it in war and in the death brought by war, an insight of especial relevance to Europe at this time. Yet these negative insights are never left to stand unopposed, as the reconciliation poems of *One Foot in Eden* show. Through them he reminds us, as does Blake, that there can be a vision of innocence, of love and human cooperation.

To the very end of his life, then, Muir pursued the three mysteries he identified in *An Autobiography*: 'where we came from, where we are going, and . . . how we should live with one another'. This discourse was conducted in poetry, in criticism and in fiction, both philo-sophically and in terms of our everyday world. Although on the whole he was not stylistically an active participant in modernism, he contributed much to our understanding of that movement by his struggles with it as man and poet. Through this creative resistance to the artistic mores of the time and through his insistence on the essential relationship between literature and society, he did much to keep alive perceptions of still meaningful traditional values which had been cast aside in the enthusiasm for the new. In the British context, his critical writings and translations of European authors such as Kafka increased public awareness of European literature, while, as with modernism, his struggles with his 'second country' Scotland have contributed much to our understanding of the fragmented Scottish cultural situation and the choices before us. In his poetry and prose-writing, he fulfilled the Scottish Renaissance aim of taking Scottish literature back into the mainstream of European culture.

For all these reasons, and in particular for the quality, insight and breadth of his late poetry, Edwin Muir seems to me to be a poet of especial relevance to our century and one whose reputation and significance will continue to grow.

NOTES

1. Daniel Hoffman, *Barbarous Knowledge: Myth in the Work of Yeats, Graves and Muir* (New York: Oxford University Press, 1967), p. 250.

2. Muir, 'Scottish Life and Letters', BBC Radio, 23 May 1954, quoted in Butter, *Man and Poet*, p. 253.
3. Graham Hough, *An Essay on Criticism* (London: Duckworth, 1966), pp. 155–6.
4. Neil M. Gunn, 'Highland Games', *Scots Magazine* XV, no 6, September 1931, p. 414. Reprinted in *The Man Who Came Back: Essays and Short Stories by Neil M. Gunn*, ed. Margery McCulloch (Edinburgh: Polygon, 1991), pp. 41-7.
5. Neil M. Gunn, *Young Art and Old Hector* (London: Faber & Faber, 1942), Souvenir Press ed. (1976), p. 251.
6. George Mackay Brown, 'The Wireless Set', *A Time to Keep* (London: Hogarth Press, 1969), pp. 100–6.
7. Robert Henryson, 'The Preiching of the Swallow', *Henryson*, selected by Hugh MacDiarmid (Harmondsworth: Penguin Books, (1973), p. 52.

Selected Bibliography

For a full bibliography of the writings of Edwin Muir, see Elgin W. Mellown, *Bibliography of the Writings of Edwin Muir* (Alabama: University of Alabama Press, 1964; revised ed. 1966; London: Nicholas Vane, 1966, 1970).

VERSE

First Poems. London: Hogarth Press, 1925.
Chorus of the Newly Dead. London: Hogarth Press, 1926.
Six Poems. Warlingham: Samson Press, 1932.
Variations on a Time Theme. London: Dent, 1934.
Journeys and Places. London: Faber & Faber, 1937.
The Narrow Place. London: Faber & Faber, 1943.
The Voyage and Other Poems. London: Faber & Faber, 1946.
The Labyrinth. London: Faber & Faber, 1949.
Collected Poems 1921–51. Ed. J. C. Hall. London: Faber & Faber, 1952.
Prometheus (Ariel Poems). Illustrated by John Piper. London: Faber & Faber, 1954.
One Foot in Eden. London: Faber & Faber, 1956.
Collected Poems 1921–58. London: Faber & Faber, 1960. Second ed., with minor alterations and addition of one poem, London: Faber & Faber, 1963.
Selected Poems. Ed. T. S. Eliot. London: Faber & Faber, 1965.
The Complete Poems of Edwin Muir. An annotated edition, ed. Peter Butter. Aberdeen: Association for Scottish Literary Studies, 1991.

PROSE

We Moderns. Under pseudonym of 'Edward Moore'. London: Allen & Unwin, 1918.
Latitudes. London: Melrose, 1924.
Transition: Essays on Contemporary Literature. London: Hogarth Press, 1926.
The Marionette. London: Hogarth Press, 1927. Paperback ed., 1987.
The Structure of the Novel. London: Hogarth Press, 1928. Chatto & Windus paperback ed., 1979.
John Knox: Portrait of a Calvinist. London: Jonathan Cape, 1929.
The Three Brothers. London: Heinemann, 1931.
Poor Tom. London: Dent, 1932. Edinburgh: Paul Harris Publishing, 1982.

Scottish Journey. London: Heinemann, 1935. Edinburgh: Mainstream
Publishing Company, 1979.
Social Credit and the Labour Party: An Appeal by Edwin Muir. London: Nott,
1935.
Scott and Scotland: The Predicament of the Scottish Writer. London: Routledge,
1936. Edinburgh: Polygon Books, 1982.
The Present Age: From 1914 (Introduction to English Literature Series, Vol. V).
London: Cresset Press, 1939.
The Story and the Fable: An Autobiography. London: Harrap, 1940.
The Scots and their Country. London: Longmans, Green & Co., 1946.
The Politics of King Lear. Glasgow: Jackson (Glasgow University Press),
1947.
Essays on Literature and Society. London: Hogarth Press, 1949. Second revised
ed. with six previously uncollected essays added, London: Hogarth Press,
1965.
An Autobiography. London: Hogarth Press, 1954.
The Estate of Poetry. London: Hogarth Press, 1962.
Selected Letters of Edwin Muir. Ed. P. H. Butter. London: Hogarth Press, 1974.
Edwin Muir: Uncollected Scottish Criticism. Ed. Andrew Noble. London: Barnes
& Noble, 1982.
Edwin Muir: Selected Prose. Chosen by George Mackay Brown. London: John
Murray, 1987.
Edwin Muir: The Truth of the Imagination: Some Uncollected Reviews and Essays.
Ed. Peter Butter. Aberdeen: Aberdeen University Press, 1988.

SOME CRITICAL STUDIES

Aitchison, James. *The Golden Harvester: The Vision of Edwin Muir*. Aberdeen:
Aberdeen University Press, 1988.
Akros. Special Edwin Muir Number. Vol. 16, no 47, August 1981.
Blackmur, R. P. 'Edwin Muir: Between the Tiger's Paws'. *Kenyon Review*
XXI, no 2, 1959, pp. 419–36.
Butter, P. H. *Edwin Muir*. Edinburgh: Oliver & Boyd, 1962.
—— *Edwin Muir: Man and Poet*. Edinburgh and London: Oliver & Boyd,
1966.
Chapman 49. 'Special Feature on Edwin Muir, 1887–1959 in Celebration of
his Centenary'. Vol. IX, no 6, Summer 1987.
Cox, C. B. 'The Horses: An Analysis'. *Critical Survey* I, no 1, Autumn
1962, pp. 19–21.
Crawford, Thomas. 'Edwin Muir as a Political Poet'. *Literature of the North*.
Ed. D. Hewitt. Aberdeen: Aberdeen University Press, 1983, pp. 121–33.
Feder, Lillian. *Ancient Myth in Modern Poetry*. Princeton: Princeton
University Press, 1971, pp. 368–77.
Gardner, Helen. *Edwin Muir: The W. D. Thomas Memorial Lecture*. Cardiff:
University of Wales Press, 1961.
Gaskill, P. H. 'Edwin Muir and Goethe'. *Proceedings of the English Goethe
Society* no 48, 1978, pp. 22–51.
—— 'Edwin Muir as Critic of Hölderlin'. *Forum for Modern Language Studies*
no 14, 1978, pp. 345–64.

—— 'Edwin Muir's Friend in Hellerau: Iwar von Lücken'. *German Life and Letters*, new series, no 32, 1978–9, pp. 135–47.

—— 'Edwin Muir: The German Aspect'. *Lines Review* no 69, June 1979, pp. 14–20.

—— Hölderlin and the Poetry of Edwin Muir'. *Forum for Modern Language Studies* no 16, 1980, pp. 12–32.

—— 'Edwin Muir in Hellerau'. *Scottish Literary Journal* no 11, May 1984, pp. 45–56.

Gunn, Neil M. Review of *Scott and Scotland* by Edwin Muir. *Scots Magazine* XXVI, no 1, October 1936, pp. 72–8.

—— Review of *The Narrow Place* by Edwin Muir. *Scots Magazine* XXXIX, no 2, May 1943, pp. 163–4.

Hoffman, Daniel. *Barbarous Knowledge: Myth in the Work of Yeats, Graves and Muir*. New York: Oxford University Press, 1967.

Holloway, John. 'The Modernity of Edwin Muir'. *The Colours of Clarity: Essays on Contemporary Literature and Education*. London: Routledge & Kegan Paul, 1964, pp. 95–112.

Huberman, Elizabeth. *The Poetry of Edwin Muir: The Field of Good and Ill*. New York: Oxford University Press, 1971.

Jennings, Elizabeth. 'Edwin Muir as Poet and Allegorist'. *London Magazine* 7, no 3, March 1960, pp. 43–56.

Knight, Roger. *Edwin Muir: An Introduction to his Work*. London: Longman, 1980.

Marshall, George. *In a Distant Isle: The Orkney Background of Edwin Muir*. Edinburgh: Scottish Academic Press, 1987.

Merwin, W. S. 'Four British Poets'. *Kenyon Review* XV, Summer 1953, pp. 461–76.

Morgan, Edwin. 'Edwin Muir'. *Essays*. Cheadle Hulme: Carcanet, 1974, pp. 188–9.

Muir, Willa. *Belonging: A Memoir*. London: Hogarth Press, 1968.

McCulloch, Margery. 'Edwin Muir's Scottish Journey 1935–80'. *Scottish Review* no 17, February 1980, pp. 47–52.

—— 'Inter-War Criticism'. *History of Scottish Literature* Vol. 4: 'Twentieth Century'. Aberdeen: Aberdeen University Press, 1987, pp. 119–32.

—— 'The Single, Disunited World: Edwin Muir and Prague'. *Scotland and the Slavs: Selected Papers from the Glasgow–90 East–West Forum*. Nottingham: Astra Press, 1993.

MacLachlan, C. J. M. and Robb, D. S. (eds). *Edwin Muir: Centenary Assessments*. Aberdeen: Association for Scottish Literary Studies, 1990.

Raine, Kathleen. 'Edwin Muir: An Appreciation'. *Texas Quarterly* IV, no 3, Autumn 1961, pp. 233–45.

Robertson, Ritchie. 'Some Revisions and Variants in the Poetry of Edwin Muir'. *Bibliotheck* 10, 1980, pp. 20–6.

—— '"Our Generation": Edwin Muir as Social Critic, 1920–22'. *Scottish Literary Journal* Vol. 9, no 2, December 1982, pp. 45–65.

—— 'Edwin Muir and Rilke'. *German Life and Letters*, new series, 36, 1982–3, pp. 317–28.

—— 'Edwin Muir as Critic of Kafka'. *Modern Language Review* Vol. 79, no 4, July 1984, pp. 638–52.

—— 'Edwin Muir'. *History of Scottish Literature* Vol. 4: 'Twentieth Century'. Aberdeen: Aberdeen University Press, 1987, pp. 135–46.

Wiseman, Christopher. *Beyond the Labyrinth: A Study of Edwin Muir's Poetry.* Victoria BC: Sono Nis Press, 1978.

Index

EU Authorised Representative:

Easy Access System Europe Mustamäe tee 50, 10621 Tallinn, Estonia

gpsr.requests@easproject.com

Printed and bound by CPI Group (UK) Ltd, Croydon, CR0 4YY

22/04/2026

02095386-0001